4x21(18)

DATE DUE

RIDING INTO BATTLE

Canadian Cyclists in the Great War

TED GLENN

DUNDURN
TORONTO

Front and back cover images: Library and Archives Canada/Ministry of the Overseas Military Forces of Canada fonds/e001131472.
Printer: Webcom

Library and Archives Canada Cataloguing in Publication

Glenn, Ted, 1960-, author
       Riding into battle : Canadian cyclists in the Great War / Ted Glenn.

Includes bibliographical references and index.
Issued in print and electronic formats.
ISBN 978-1-4597-4261-1 (softcover).--ISBN 978-1-4597-4262-8 (PDF).--
ISBN 978-1-4597-4263-5 (EPUB)

       1. Canada. Canadian Army. Canadian Corps. Cyclist Battalion.
2. Military cycling--Canada--History--20th century. 3. World War,
1914-1918--Regimental histories--Canada. I. Title.

UH35.C3G64 2018   357'.523097109041   C2018-902662-6
                                                     C2018-902663-4

1 2 3 4 5   22 21 20 19 18

Conseil des Arts du Canada   Canada Council for the Arts   Canada   ONTARIO ARTS COUNCIL
CONSEIL DES ARTS DE L'ONTARIO
an Ontario government agency
un organisme du gouvernement de l'Ontario

We acknowledge the support of the Canada Council for the Arts, which last year invested $153 million to bring the arts to Canadians throughout the country, and the Ontario Arts Council for our publishing program. We also acknowledge the financial support of the Government of Ontario, through the Ontario Book Publishing Tax Credit and the Ontario Media Development Corporation, and the Government of Canada.

Nous remercions le Conseil des arts du Canada de son soutien. L'an dernier, le Conseil a investi 153 millions de dollars pour mettre de l'art dans la vie des Canadiennes et des Canadiens de tout le pays.

VISIT US AT

dundurn.com | @dundurnpress | dundurnpress | dundurnpress

Dundurn
3 Church Street, Suite 500
Toronto, Ontario, Canada
M5E 1M2

For the 1,138 Canadian Cyclists who enlisted to fight in the Great War, including the 261 who were killed or wounded

And for Dick Ellis, who worked tirelessly to keep the Cyclists' Great War legacy alive

It was during the last 100 days when "Heine" was being pushed back that the Cyclists really functioned as such. At this time every fourth man carried a Lewis Gun on his bicycle.... Time and again our lads were sent out far in advance of the infantry to keep touch with the retreating enemy and many were the tales of heroism and sacrifice recorded that make us very proud of the unit in which we served. The Cyclist Battalion cast off their role of Corps handymen and Engineer's navvies and assumed the character for which their training had fitted them.

— Captain Dick Ellis

They were typical Canadian Cyclists to a man. They lived hard — fought hard — and died hard, when they came to it.

— from *Saga of the Cyclists in the Great War, 1914–1918*

It is well for our mental welfare that we could see the humorous side, otherwise our memories of strenuous days between 1914 and 1918 would be a constant night-mare rather than pleasant recollections.

— Private Tobias Kelly

Contents

Introduction

The last hundred days of the Great War started with the Battle of Amiens on August 8, 1918. For Canadian soldiers, preparations began nine days earlier under the cover of darkness. The Canadians by that time had become renowned on both sides of the Western Front as elite shock troops, called on by the British to lead particularly difficult assignments (like Vimy and Hill 70 the year before) and feared by the Germans for their successes. To keep the impending offensive — and Canada's role in it — secret, the entire Canadian Corps made the nearly 40-mile move from their positions at Arras to staging areas west of Amiens over the course of nine short, hot nights beginning on July 30.[1]

The range of Canadian battlefield technologies on parade through the French countryside that summer included older ones like infantry, cavalry, and heavy artillery, and newer ones like motorized machine-gun lorries, armoured cars — and 300 bicycles. On July 31, Cyclists with the Canadian Corps Cyclist Battalion set out at 22:00 for a short one mile ride from Arras to a rendezvous point at Gézaincourt. After resting up and "lying low all day,"[2] the Cyclists pedalled hard for seven hours to the Canadians' main staging area west of Amiens at Thieulloy-l'Abbaye.[3] The Battalion's official war diary recorded the Cyclists arriving at 06:00 on the morning of August 2, "very tired having ridden 57 kilometres."[4]

Their exhaustion is not surprising — the full Cyclist kit in the Great War weighed in at almost 90 pounds.[5] Captain Dick Ellis,[6] who served with "B" Cyclist Company, recalled the night rides of the "famous secret move to the Amiens front" as "excellent conditioners for cycling muscles and the second night in particular, when the Battalion covered 57 kilometres in pitch darkness, was a real test of stamina and discipline."[7]

At Amiens, the Canadian Corps was assigned a nearly 5,500-yard front extending from the Amiens–Chaulnes railway near Villers-Bretonneux on the north to the Amiens–Roye road at Hourges on the south (see Map 1, page 13). The 2nd Canadian Division was positioned on the left of the front (with the Australian Corps on its northern flank), the 3rd Division on the right (with the French First Army on its southern flank), and the 1st Division in the middle. The 4th Canadian Division was placed in reserve, ready to be brought forward later in the offensive (see Map 2, page 14).

Canadian Corps commander Lieutenant General Arthur Currie's plan for the Amiens offensive was relatively simple: begin with a massive early-morning artillery barrage to dislodge German defences and provide cover for infantry to attack the enemy's outpost positions along a so-called Green Line. With this first objective achieved, tanks would then advance through the infantry to crush the enemy's main defensive positions guarded by machine-gun nests. This Red Line objective ran from the village of Harbonnières north of the railway to the village of Mézières south of the Amiens–Roye road. If successful, the cavalry would then be called in to execute a final high-speed advance for a Blue Line objective, the French army's old Outer Amiens Defence Line from 1916 now serving as the enemy's rear defence area and including its main artillery positions. Currie's plan would see the Canadians moving across a landscape scarred by the battles of the previous four years — shattered villages, old trench systems, massive shell holes, blasted roadways, and ruined bridges.

One wrinkle in Currie's plan was a scheduled 45-minute delay to the start of the French army's advance to the south of the Amiens–Roye road.[8] The delay would make the 3rd Canadian Division's southern flank vulnerable to attack until the French could catch up. To protect this "soft southern underbelly,"[9] particularly during the cavalry stage of the offensive, Currie created the Canadian Independent Force (CIF), a mobile

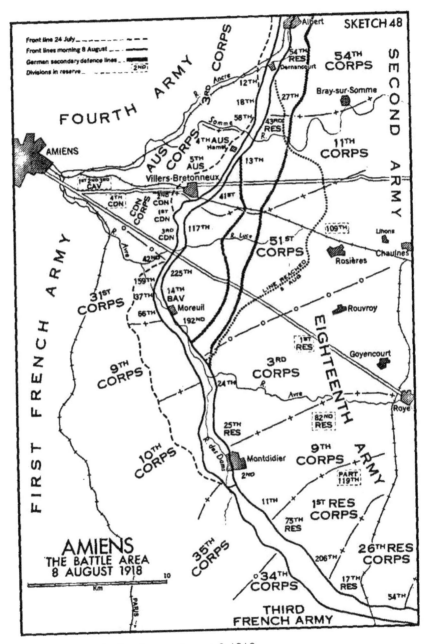

Map 1: Amiens, the battle area, August 8, 1918.

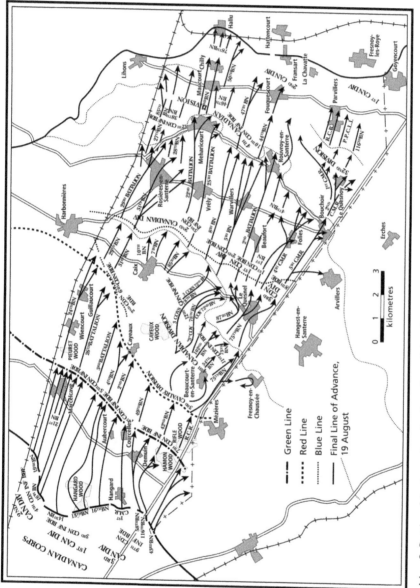

Map 2: Battle of Amiens, showing location of the Canadian Divisions.

brigade that could move independently up and down the Amiens–Roye road as needed until the Canadian and French lines could conform.

The CIF, under the command of Brigadier-General Raymond Brutinel, was organized into six mobile units: one trench mortar section with two Newton Mortar–outfitted lorries (the Trench Mortar Section), one armoured car detachment with four cars and one platoon of Cyclists (the Armoured Car Detachment), two motor-machine-gun brigades each with five 40-gun batteries and two platoons of Cyclists (Nos. 1 and 2 Groups), another armoured car detachment with two cars and four platoons of Cyclists (No. 3 Group), and a supply section to give the Force the ammunition, fuel, water, rations, and first aid needed to function on its own.[10] The CIF represented the Canadian Corps's most advanced thinking about and experience with combined arms and mobile warfare, and it was with the CIF (and its various incarnations over the Hundred Days campaign) that Canadian Cyclists made their unique and most significant contributions to the Great War.

Positioned behind the 3rd Canadian Division along the Amiens–Roye road on the morning of August 8, the CIF had orders to pass through the 3rd Division infantry after it achieved its Red Line objective and "[make] good the line" between positions held by the advancing

Line-up of cyclists parading next to the Autocars purchased by Brutinel.

3rd Canadian Cavalry Division and the French to the south of the Amiens–Roye road.[11] As fighting progressed and the Canadian-French line conformed, the CIF were ordered to be ready "to exploit success down the Roye road."[12]

ZERO HOUR

The start of the Battle of Amiens — zero hour — was set for 04:20 on August 8, 1918. In preparation, Brutinel's CIF rendezvoused at Gentelles Road at 01:00. As 3rd Canadian Division infantry moved forward behind their creeping artillery barrage, the CIF readied to advance down the Amiens–Roye road at 05:00. At 07:33, the entire CIF moved out, passing through the village of Domart at 09:10 and then setting up HQ at the intersection of the Amiens–Roye and Démuin–Moreuil roads.

From HQ, the armoured car detachment under the command of Captain Roy Clark set off for the village of Maison Blanche to "get in touch with the enemy."[13] The four cars and single platoon of Cyclists (No. 8 Platoon) passed through the infantry of the Royal Canadian Regiment who were positioned on the left of the Amiens–Roye road and the French infantry who had caught up on the right. One section of Cyclists took the lead in guard formation, the remaining three following at 100-yard intervals, with the armoured cars bringing up the rear. The detachment cleared out a sniper's nest near the road and then rolled into Maison Blanche at 10:00. While the village itself had been cleared by infantry, the detachment came under heavy machine-gun fire from the direction of Mézières, another village farther to the southeast. Clark ordered two cars and one section of Cyclists to investigate. The troops ran into a German gun crew at a cemetery on the northern outskirts of the village and opened fire. After a short exchange, the Allied soldiers captured a field gun and took 30 prisoners.

Meanwhile, to the south of Mézières, gun battery "E" from CIF No. 1 Group advanced to a position where they could keep enemy forces in the village under fire while French infantry began their infiltration. They didn't get far — the cluster of German machine guns to the east of the village opened up and kept the French advance "to a dribble."[14] Seeing the situation unfold, gun battery "C" from No. 1 Group travelled farther east in an effort to outflank the Germans and force the machine gunners to surrender to the French. One section of Cyclists provided cover for the gunners here "in a very skillful manner and by Rifle Fire inflicted heavy casualties on the enemy."[15]

At about 14:00, the French with the support of Walker's armoured car detachment captured the village of Mézières. Task accomplished, Walker's detachment set off down the Amiens–Roye road with cavalry and whippet tanks on their left. It got as far as a chalk pit south of Beaucourt, where it encountered enemy machine-gun fire and hand grenades. The detachment returned enough fire to proceed another 300 yards down the road before running into much heavier machine-gun fire from both left and right. The detachment dug in here, near the intersection with the Le Quesnel–Fresnoy-en-Chaussée road, and waited for help.

The first unit ordered forward to help was machine-gun battery "A" with two sections of Cyclists from No. 5 Platoon. This unit had begun its day at 08:15 with instructions to "maintain contact with the enemy" — or, in Cyclist Private Allan Macnab's words, "chase Fritz up the Amiens-Roye road all day."[16] It made first contact with the enemy southeast of Beaucort at about 11:00. There, four of the Cyclists were sent forward to reconnoitre the village. Despite running into heavy machine-gun fire, they returned to the main unit without casualty. Another four Cyclists were sent off to reconnoitre the road toward Le Quesnel and found more Germans dug in a half-mile west of the village. Cyclist Sergeant Frederick Wingfield described the action there like this:

> I was detailed to take three men and reconnoitre the main road in the direction of Le Quesnel and I found the enemy holding the woods about a kilometre west of Le Quesnel with strong machine gun posts. I sent a report to "A" Battery and armoured cars were sent up and I pointed out some enemy positions but they could not dislodge them all. The enemy brought up artillery and the armoured cars and my section had to retire below

A Canadian armoured car going into action, Battle of Amiens.

the crest of the hill. Pte Andrew was knocked down by a bursting shell and slightly wounded in the left fore-arm, but he did not report to Field Ambulance.[17]

Wingfield and his Cyclists returned to the main unit, made their report, and went out again accompanying some of the armoured cars to identify more enemy machine-gun positions. Macnab recalled that the Cyclists "finally ran into [German] reserves about 5:00 p.m. He held us in a sunken road just short of Le Quesnel about 6 miles from our starting point."[18] This was the place where the "A," "B," and "C" machine-gun batteries and the Cyclist companies met up with an armoured car detachment and set up defensive positions for the night. The remainder of the CIF moved to HQ's new position just east of Maison Blanche for the night as well.

For the CIF, the night of August 8 would offer short respite — zero hour on August 9 was set for 04:00 and the CIF's first order of business would be to help 3rd Canadian Division infantry capture the heavily defended village of Le Quesnel.

RIDING INTO BATTLE

This book tells the untold story of Canadian Cyclists in the Great War. Chapter 1 begins back in Canada — at Valcartier Camp north of Quebec City, Camp Exhibition in Toronto, and Paradise Grove at Niagara-on-the-Lake — where the five original divisional Cyclist companies were organized and put through basic training between September 1914 and April 1916. As then-Private Ken Pettis recalled, "If our training bore little relationship to the type of warfare then being waged in France, where so-called 'mounted troops' were fighting grimly in the trenches of Sanctuary Wood, it was interesting training anyhow!"[19] Chapter 1 follows the Cyclists to England, where Canadian volunteers took advanced training related to their specialties — machine gun, signal, cook, field ambulance, Cyclist. On manoeuvres one morning near camp at Shorncliffe, the future premier of Ontario, Major Thomas Laird Kennedy, learned the hard way that advanced training could be as treacherous as fighting at the front. Leading his company of nearly two hundred Cyclists down an enormous, conical hill near camp "on almost a free wheel,"[20] Kennedy "rounded the second hairpin turn near the bottom … [and] ran smack into a truck, landing up on the front seat. In addition to many bad cuts and bruises, his jaw was broken, completely destroying any claim he previously had to beauty."[21]

For most of the Great War, Canadian Cyclists performed few of the specialized duties they were trained for. Mostly, they were assigned to "patrolling of roads, regulation of traffic, and supplying working parties for digging trenches and other earth works."[22] Chapter 2 summarizes the work of the Cyclists in this period by focusing on three famous battles: Ypres in 1915, where the Cyclists were reduced to "tying a wet sock over our mouth and nose" as they had "no gas masks or steel helmets";[23] the Somme in 1916, where Cyclists' work "consisted largely of carrying ammunition and other supplies, burying cable, and other digging parties, with the odd turn at stretcher-bearing and burying the dead bodies scattered around all over";[24] and Vimy in 1917, where Cyclists' primary job was "putting most of Vimy Ridge in sand bags."[25]

The Canadian Cyclists' greatest contributions to the Great War began at the Battle of Amiens in August 1918 and continued through the Hundred

Brigadier-General Raymond Brutinel in military uniform.

Days campaign. As Cyclist Lance Corporal Allan Macnab put it, at Amiens the "Cyclists finally came into their own. The open warfare gave them a chance to carry out the work for which they were enlisted."[26] Chapter 3 picks up where this introduction leaves off, with the Cyclists at the Battle of Amiens (August 8–11). While the Canadian Independent Force met its immediate tactical objectives there, Brigadier-General Brutinel believed the Force ultimately fell short of making "full use of the power of manoeuvre."[27]

The shortcomings Brutinel observed at Amiens came to a head at the Canadian Corps's next engagements at Arras and the Drocourt-Quéant (D-Q) Line (August 26–September 3), the subject of Chapter 4. For General Currie, the fighting there by the Canadian Corps was "one of the finest performances in all the war."[28] Cyclists and the Independent Force, however, failed to achieve their primary objective: securing the bridgeheads on the Canal du Nord at Marquion. Brutinel laid blame on the Force's ad hoc status. For him, its "spasmodic extemporarity" had prevented it from training together, "learn[ing] their possibilities and limitations, acquir[ing] mutual confidence and unity of purpose."[29] Brutinel was persuasive: on September 19, Currie issued orders to establish the Force — now called Brutinel's Brigade — on a permanent basis.

The first test of Brutinel's now-permanent brigade came at the Canal du Nord (September 27–October 1) and Cambrai (October 9–11). Chapter 5 describes how the break allowed the Corps as a whole — Brutinel's Brigade specifically — to undertake specialized training for the looming and highly technical offensive. Brutinel and his staff developed a customized two-week training program that stressed "the necessity of close cooperation with the other Batteries and all Arms of the Service" — i.e., the machine gun and trench mortar batteries, armoured cars, motorcyclists, Cyclists, and a new addition to the brigade, the Canadian Light Horse cavalry regiment. While Brutinel's Brigade was not engaged in the opening sequences of the offensive at the Canal du Nord (owing to the "sticky fighting" from the German's "very determined resistance"),[30] the troops, including the Cyclists, did demonstrate a "fine spirit of comradeship and co-operation" in the pursuit of German forces following the capture of Cambrai on October 9. This "noteworthy performance"[31] is the subject of Chapter 6.

The Canadian Corps's pursuit of the retreating Germans from Cambrai ended temporarily at the l'Escaut and Sensée canals on October 11, 1918. Chapter 7 describes how, after six days' rest and recalibration, the Corps crossed the canals and resumed the chase of the crumbling German army, a phase of the Hundred Days campaign known as the Pursuit from the Sensée Canal (October 17–23). This, in Cyclist Allan Macnab's estimation, was the Canadian Cyclists' "most telling work,"[32] providing "reconnaissance patrols for the two attacking divisions," keeping in "constant touch with the enemy as it retreated," "communicating enemy positions and anything else of importance like road and bridge status to the infantry coming behind," and providing "runners to keep brigade HQs connected as they advanced over the open territory."[33] At the end of the Pursuit, Major-General Sir David Watson (commander of the 4th Canadian Division) expressed his "appreciation of the valuable assistance rendered us" by Brutinel's Brigade, including the Cyclists whom he singled out for their "valuable and excellent Patrol duties [that] kept us constantly in touch with the enemy carrying out this hazardous work with great skill and complete satisfaction."[34]

Chapter 8 explores Canadian Cyclists' role in Canada's last two offensives of the Great War, the major battle at Valenciennes (November 1–2) and the minor one involved in the capture of Mons (November 10–11). At Valenciennes, the guns of Brutinel's Brigade were deployed to support the 4th Canadian Division's massive artillery barrage, the Cyclists and cavalry troops employed as dispatch riders, runners, and orderlies "between Headquarters of Brigades and the advanced Battalion Headquarters and also for keeping up Communication between the Scouts, Patrols, Companies and Infantry Report Centres."[35] In the final push to Mons, the brigade was retooled into a two-detachment force, responsible for "advancing through the Infantry and working ahead of them" if the enemy's "line of resistance was broken or its rearguard pierced."[36] While the infantry of the 2nd Division made excellent progress over the four-day march to Mons, the almost complete demolition of the roads brought Brutinel's mobile units — including the Cyclists — effectively to a halt for this last phase of the war.

The capture of Mons on the morning of November 11 and the signing of the armistice did not end the Great War for Canadians serving in it. As Chapter 9 describes, the 1st and 2nd Canadian Divisions, along with the Canadian Corps Cyclist Battalion, were assigned to represent Canada in the Allied occupying force following the signing of the armistice. As they had at Valenciennes and Mons, the Cyclists performed advance and flank patrol duties on the 250-mile march to the Rhine, sometimes riding up to a day in advance of the main columns. They also performed guard duty while encamped, which involved "selecting the Out-post Line and occupying this until relieved by the Infantry of the Advance Guard."[37]

The Canadians encountered an almost completely different world on the march to the Rhine — a landscape largely untouched by the war, towns and villages intact. The streams of war prisoners they passed, though, brought the horrors of the past four years back into stark relief. According to Ellis, "No transportation had been arranged for them and hitch-hiking facilities were not very good going west. Many of them were in a pitiful condition. We could only hope that when they got behind our columns they would be well taken care of.[38] Chapter 9 concludes the book with the story of Privates William Oborne and Arthur Wardell, Cyclists released from German internment on November 17, 1918.

Ultimately, this book aims to fill a gap in the history of Canada's role in the Great War by chronicling the work of Canadian Cyclists in it. As argued in the epilogue, the Cyclists' legacy is based on and bound up with the pioneering contributions made by the Canadian Independent Force/ Brutinel's Brigade to the Hundred Days campaign, specifically as they relate to the development of the Canadian Corps's combined arms strategy, mobile warfare doctrine, and consummate professionalism. The cost of that legacy, now largely forgotten, was steep: out of a total enlistment of 1,138 men, 261 were killed or wounded — a casualty rate of 23 percent.[39] No wonder the Cyclists, like many other units in the Great War, referred to their battalion as the "Suicide Squad."[40] This is their story.

1

Battle of the Humber

1ST CANADIAN DIVISIONAL CYCLIST COMPANY

On August 5, 1914, Canadian governor general H.R.H. the Duke of Connaught announced that Canada would follow Britain into war with Germany. Within days, Minister of Militia and Defence Sam Hughes issued a call-to-arms and raised a fighting force of more than 30,000 volunteer troops; an estimated 5,000 more than that made their way to the newly created training camp at Valcartier, Quebec, in early September. "Accommodations at Valcartier," recalled one Cyclist, "left much to be desired, particularly at the outset as practically a new camp had to be set up, including four miles of Bell tents for sleeping purposes."[1] With surprising speed, the basic logistics of camp life were sorted out — tents erected, water lines installed, latrines dug, mess organized, rifle and artillery ranges built.

Once the volunteers were assembled at Valcartier, senior command of the First Canadian Contingent turned to organizing them into a fighting force. The Canadians followed British practice and established both regimented units like infantry[2] and specialized "troop" units like engineering and medical units that reported directly to divisional command.

A Highland regiment waiting to have supplies allotted before leaving Valcartier Camp, Quebec, 1915.

Amongst the latter was the 1st Divisional Mounted Troops, a unit made up of the 196-member Cavalry Service Squadron (drawn from the 19th Alberta Dragoons) and the 93-member 1st Canadian Divisional Cyclist Company drawn from general volunteers at Valcartier.[3]

Since the Boer War,[4] cyclists had been paired with cavalry units to carry out duties that required troops to dismount.[5] The thinking was that the "act of dismounting deprived a cavalry unit of the services of the men detailed to care for the horses. As one man could only manage four horses or so, the transition from saddle to boot cost a cavalry unit some 25 percent of its rifle strength. A cyclist unit, however, did not have to worry about its mounts running off on their own accord or being hit by stray small-arms fire."[6] Cyclists were generally trained to perform a range of duties across the battlefield.[7] In an advance, cyclists were trained to "find the enemy out for the infantry [and] keep in touch and warn the infantry of the proximity, and, if possible, strength of the enemy." Behind the trenches, cyclists were trained to patrol roads, regulate military traffic, secure important bridgeworks and crossings, guard prisoners, and support divisional communications as dispatch riders. In addition, cyclists were expected to perform a range of other duties as required, including "orderly duties," "seeking out of spies and watching suspects," and "supplying working parties for digging trenches and other earth works."[8]

The 1st Division Cyclists had only two weeks to train as a company before marching to Quebec City for embarkation to England on October 3.[9] As with most volunteers' experiences at Valcartier, though, much of their time was "spent in filling out forms and undergoing inoculations that left everyone sick for several days."[10] This was certainly the Cyclists' experience. As one recalled, "There was little opportunity for any special training in the short time to go prior to embarkation for England — in fact, the comparatively short stay of all units in Valcartier did not allow much opportunity for any organized training. This was confined mainly to platoon and company drill with a few route marches and some target practice."[11] And there was only "the odd bicycle" available to train on; the Cyclists were not supplied with their own bicycles until arriving at Salisbury Plain in England in October.[12]

QUAGMIRE

After waiting onboard the SS *Ruthenia* for more than a week for transport, the 1st Division Cyclists arrived at Pond Farm, Salisbury Plain, about 75 miles southwest of London (near Stonehenge), on October 14. Salisbury, like other camps across Britain, had been established to train the Empire's volunteer army under the command of the Earl of Kitchener. Side by side with recruits from Britain, Australia, and New Zealand, the "camps were bursting at the seams with Canadians. We had barely arrived when the rain started to fall and kept falling during our whole stay. We soon lived in a quagmire. At times the rain even penetrated the canvas of the tents while they were standing. Quite often they fell, as it was difficult to anchor the ropes in the mud. However, the boys were young and full of pep and it took a lot to get them down."[13]

A Canadian Cyclist on post in the flooded Salisbury Plain.

To "counteract the effect of the mud and rain," the Cyclists and other soldiers made forays to pubs in the town of Salisbury, other surrounding towns, and even London as the canteens at camp were initially dry.[14] According to one Cyclist, "Quite often this was without a pass — something of which the Military Police did not exactly approve when they caught up with us, and the escapades of some of the more unruly individuals which were not really too wild, tended to give Canadians a bad name. We were sometimes referred to as 'Kitchener's Canadian Mob.'"[15]

The incredibly wet weather (it rained 89 of the 123 days the First Contingent spent at Salisbury)[16] and disarray attendant to organizing the logistics of a massive war effort prevented much in the way of productive training at Salisbury.[17] Cyclists Major Clayton Bush and Commanding Sergeant Major Fred Delavigne recalled, "There did not appear to be any set drill for Cyclists at that time — some of the officers wanted dismounted Cavalry Drill and others Infantry Drill — but they finally settled for Cavalry and as it eventually transpired, came nearer the requirements."[18]

And even when bikes were finally issued, "the mud at Larkhill was so terrible during the remainder of October and ensuing months that cycling was out of the question most of the time."[19]

Most members of the 1st Divisional Cyclist Company were issued the Birmingham Small Arms Company (B.S.A.) Mark IV bicycle. It had been approved for British military use in 1911 and was the most common bicycle used by British, Canadian, Australian, and New Zealand forces in the Great War.[20,21] The 24-inch machine was officially a "General Service" bicycle outfitted with coaster hubs, mudguards, lamp, front and rear pannier carriers, and a repair kit with spanners, tire repair kit, and a screwdriver.[22] Also standard issue were clips for mounting a .303 Hotchkiss Portable Machine Gun "over the handlebar (for short distances when going into action)" and another for carrying the gun "through the frame for long distances, on the march."[23]

A Cyclist of Brutinel's Brigade, at Rockliffe (Ottawa) on the occasion of the governor general's inspection.

Full kit for the Cyclists included the following items:

Bicycle	Coat	Iron rations
Cap	Pullthrough	2 gas helmets
Steel helmet	Oil bottle	Goggles
Tunic	6 oz oil tin	Satchel
Pants	Web equipment	Capsules
Puttees	120 rounds	Housewife
Boots	ammunition	Hold-all
Socks (2 pairs)	Haversack	Razor
Underwear	Water bottle	Comb
Great Coat	Mess tin	Brush
Rubber cape	Entrenching tool	Knife
Blanket (1)	Handle	Fork
Ground sheet	Bayonet	Spoon
Rifle	Kitbag	Clasp knife

In addition to official kit, most of the Cyclists also had "a certain amount of personal and extra stuff, including souvenirs.... When fully loaded our cycles weighed almost 90 pounds."[24]

One month after moving to the permanent Royal Artillery Barracks at Bulford in January 1915 ("quite an improvement on the tents," recalled one Cyclist),[25] and two weeks after a final review by the King on February 4, the First Canadian Contingent, including the 1st Divisional Cyclist Company, was sent to the front lines of the Great War.

Bush and Delavigne paint a good picture of the Cyclists' arrival:

> You should have seen the fun when we landed in France. We were already loaded up with Infantry kit strapped to our Cycles, including rifles and then were issued with rain-cape and jerkin, so when that was put on top of everything, it was more like trying to mount a hay-stack than a bicycle, and to make things tougher, we undertook to ride on a greasy pave road. Men and bikes

spilled all over the place and we finally had to walk, pushing the cycles on the long trek to the Bethune area which was our ultimate destination.[26]

It didn't take long before the Cyclists and the rest of the First Contingent were "introduced to the evils of war — homes ruined by shell fire, fields full of shell holes and gashed by trenches and women struggling to 'keep the home fires burning' in the absence of their men folk at the front."[27]

2ND CANADIAN DIVISIONAL CYCLIST COMPANY

Just as the 1st Divisional Cyclist Company was shipping out for England in the fall of 1914, the Canadian government responded to Britain's call for more troops and issued a second call-to-arms to raise volunteers for a 2nd Canadian Division. Modelled on the First Contingent, the 2nd had both regimented and troop units, including a divisional mounted troops unit that housed the 2nd Divisional Cyclist Company.

Raised in October 1914 and shipped to England in June 1915, 2nd Division Cyclists were billeted in Toronto at Exhibition Camp, just west of the downtown core on the shores of Lake Ontario. The Company itself was a "very cosmopolitan crew,"[28] with platoons raised from Toronto, Montreal, Kingston, Vancouver, Winnipeg, and Halifax. And like the rest of the Canadian Corps in the Great War, a good number of recruits were newcomers to Canada: "around two-thirds of those at the Exhibition Grounds were born out of Canada — most of them in the British Isles, but some in Australia, South Africa, India, Japan, France, Channel Islands, Jamaica, and the USA."[29]

The basic training regimen for 2nd Division Cyclists was more evolved than it was for 1st Division Cyclists. It consisted of "squad drill, P.T., musketry and bayonet drill, map reading, scouting, simple signaling and route marches, with specialized training for a signal section made up of one or two men from each platoon."[30] And just before Christmas, the bicycles arrived. As 2nd Division Cyclists Corporal Ken Baillie and Private Aylmer Swinnerton recalled, "Needless to say, Toronto winters

No. 9 Platoon, Cyclist Corps, Exhibition Camp, Toronto, Ontario.

Cyclist Corps.

Cyclist Corps at Camp Exhibition.

are a bit severe for outdoor training and particularly for cycling. All will have a vivid memory of our first ride along the ice-covered pavements — many were the spills, the curses, and the bruises — but the thrill of the new bikes offset it all and that evening we whistled Colonel Bogey as cheerfully as ever as we marched down to our Mess Hall under the Exhibition Grandstand."[31]

BATTLE OF THE HUMBER

With spring, 2nd Division recruits stationed at Exhibition Camp headed outside for manoeuvres. A recurring drill, which most recruits stationed at Exhibition Camp over the Great War took part in, was the "Battle of the Humber," designed to "give the officers in charge a chance of handling their forces under active service conditions."[32] The *Globe* covered one iteration of the "battle" involving more than 2,000 soldiers, including the 2nd Division Cyclists, in March 1915:

> The scheme consisted of a rear attack on a fairly strong enemy. The enemy was supposed to be retreating from the city to the east, his forces consisting of the Mounted Rifle Regiment, one battery of artillery with two guns, and one company of the 19th Battalion. The offensive force was composed of the 10th Battalion, two batteries of artillery and the Divisional Cyclist Corps. The scene of the engagement covered a space of some three square miles, three-quarters of a mile on each side of the Old Mill.
>
> On reaching the river the retreating force found that the offensive had burned the bridges and orders were sent out to the rear guard to hold the attacking force in check until the crossing could be negotiated. In the wooded section of the battle ground the Divisional Cyclists were engaged with the 19th Battalion Company from the first, but were forced back across the railway track before the main body of the 20th Battalion and artillery came up.

Cyclists on a road in Humber Valley, Ontario.

Cyclist Corps at physical exercises, Humber Valley, Ontario.

The result of the engagement was a draw. The western or attacking force had to drive in the eastern or retreating force. They did so, but the eastern force delayed the process long enough to enable them to achieve their object.[33]

Not all manoeuvres along the Humber were entirely military in nature. On march through the valley at some point in early 1915, Cyclist Jock Farquhar recalled a group of the Cyclists finding "a lot of people tobogganing down the bank on to the river. We got hold of a couple of them and piled on. Well, the first one went down alright and we were doing the same until some mutt's bayonet got under one side of the rig and over we went."[34]

BELOVED MAJOR KENNEDY

On another manoeuvre in April, 2nd Division Cyclists pedalled west to Cooksville (in present-day Mississauga) to the family farm of the company's "beloved" second-in-command Major Thomas Laird Kennedy, future premier of Ontario.[35] At the farm, the Cyclists served as an "attacking force" with orders to capture a "brickyard held by a party of 50."[36]

Major Thomas Laird Kennedy pictured with his men at camp on the Cooksville Fair Grounds, Ontario, 1914.

Major T.L. Kennedy demonstrates the art of slicing a suspended lemon while galloping on horseback. He trained recruits at the Cooksville Fair Grounds in 1914.

After "a very pleasant day," the company made the 14-mile ride back to Exhibition Camp "in one hour and fourteen minutes, exemplifying our value as a mobile force. This speed of locomotion exceeds any that could be made by cavalry."[37]

Kennedy was like many officers in the Great War — he was older (35 years old at enlistment) and had served for many years in a local militia. Kennedy was born on the family farm near present-day Tomken Road[38] and Dundas Street West in Mississauga. In 1899, Kennedy began his life long career in politics when he was nominated to the local public school board "almost as a joke," recalled another future Ontario premier, Bill Davis.[39] He was elected to municipal council three years later, serving in that capacity until the war. In 1904, Kennedy also joined a local militia unit, the mounted Governor General's Body Guard, whose patron was the wealthy Denison family of west-end Toronto.[40] The GGBG (a.k.a. "Toronto's cavalry") had a long, celebrated military history, having served in the Upper Canada Rebellion, the North-West Rebellion, the Fenian raids, and the Boer War. While militia were not activated for duty in the Great War, the GGBG, like other units across the country, was active in local recruiting, both from local volunteers and within their own ranks. Kennedy

Colonel Denison of the Cyclist Corps.

and the GGBG's commander, George Taylor Denison IV, enlisted in early December 1914, with direction to establish a mounted unit. Denison was made Lieutenant-Colonel in charge of the 2nd Divisional Cyclist Company with Major Kennedy as his second-in-command.

A first draft of the 2nd Division Cyclists set sail for England in May 1915, followed by a second in early June.

SHORNCLIFFE

With the decision in early 1915 to add three more divisions to Canada's Great War effort, larger — and better appointed — training facilities were required in England. In April 1915, the Canadian Training Division was formed at Shorncliffe near Dover; at the end of May the first draft of the 2nd Division Cyclists arrived there.

Training at Shorncliffe in the summer of 1915 could not have been more different than at Salisbury Plain the autumn before. For one thing, it was sunny and warm. For another, the Cyclists were able to train on bicycles. "The training here was along pretty much the same lines as in Toronto, except less squad drills and with more long rides.... Just to show how tough his boys were Lieut. Fatt of Vancouver Platoon pushed his boys one day to a 65-mile ride in about four hours."[41] The Cyclists were also "introduced to entrenching for the first time"[42] — a skill they would hone over the next three years.

On their long, sunny rides, 2nd Division Cyclists took in the "grand and ancient sites"[43] of the English countryside — Canterbury Cathedral, Arundel Castle, the beautiful seaside village of Folkestone. They also took in the site of a group of "bathing beauties" in one-piece swimming suits:

> We had a big pile-up riding along the beach near Hythe one morning when the boys were introduced to ladies swimming in one-piece bathing suits. Up to that time bathing beauties in Canada wore as many clothes in swimming as they did on the streets just prior to the Second World War. It is doubtful if even the Colonel himself kept his eyes front as we passed them but, of course, he didn't have to keep his eyes on the bicycle ahead: many the front wheel that had to be straightened before we got under way again![44]

Front wheels were not the only casualties at Shorncliffe. One drawback of Dibgate Camp, where the Cyclists were stationed, was a steep, conical hill called Caesar's Camp, a continuation of the white chalk cliffs of Dover and purportedly the site of the first Roman camp in England.[45] "It was a real test of strength to stay on one's bike right over the top. Only a few achieved this — mostly the lighter ones."[46] It was on this hill that "our beloved Major Kennedy came to grief. He usually led us down the hill on almost a free wheel and one morning as he rounded the second hairpin turn near the bottom, he ran smack into a truck, landing up on the front seat. In addition to many bad cuts and bruises, his jaw was broken, completely destroying any claim he previously had to beauty. It was two or three months before he returned to us."[47]

3RD CANADIAN DIVISIONAL CYCLIST COMPANY

Recruitment for a 3rd Canadian Division, including a 3rd Divisional Cyclist Company, began in August 1915. Recruiters advertised for "men with a fair education … as some knowledge of map reading is desirable.

84th Overseas Battalion, Canadian Expeditionary Force, Niagara Camp.

2nd Division Cyclists, Niagara Camp.

Young fellows who have had experience in surveying, engineering or such office work as is performed by bank clerks have proved useful men in the Cyclist Corps."[48] At the end of August, Cyclist Corporal Eric Heathcoat recalled riders from "Winnipeg, London, Vancouver, Ottawa and Calgary"[49] assembling with those from Toronto and, together with "some 15 other units, mostly infantry,"[50] were shipped across Lake Ontario to camp at Paradise Grove, an area just west of Fort Niagara at Niagara-on-the-Lake.[51] Here, "the men were whipped into good shape with drilling, route marches and running."[52]

A GOOD MANY ORIGINAL AND NASTY IDEAS

The move back to Exhibition Camp in Toronto at the end of October was a highlight for the 3rd Division Cyclists. Rather than shipping back, HQ designed a manoeuvre that combined training with a long, 90-mile

march around the end of Lake Ontario. Cyclist Private Tobias Kelly recalled, "Camps were set up at various points approximately 15 miles apart, in which the battalions [one departing Niagara for Toronto each day] rested on successive nights. Each unit marched with vanguards out to hunt out the enemy, who for the purpose of these manoeuvers were our loyal Cyclists. We had separate camps established some distance off the main highway at Grimsby, Sheridan and Cooksville."[53]

Cyclist Captain George Scroggie picked up the story from this point: "The Canadian Cyclists ... were then to test the troops marching through by taking action in some form while they were approaching their billets for the night, while they were staying there at night and when they were leaving in the morning."[54] According to Scroggie, the Cyclists' main task was to "annoy each battalion after dark when it had bedded down for the night. A good many original and nasty ideas were used to accomplish these objectives and, undoubtedly, were responsible for making the Cyclists unpopular with the Infantry boys who had their rest disturbed after a strenuous day's march, by fireworks and other such annoyances."[55,56]

Back in Toronto, HQ designed one final outdoor manoeuvre before winter set in. This one, covered by the *Toronto Daily Star*, extended

Advance guard of batteries on a march from Niagara Camp to Bronte, Ontario.

Cyclists on scout duty in St. Catharines, Ontario.

beyond the city limits — from Mimico on the west to Leaside Junction on the east — and included troops from both the western Exhibition Camp and the eastern Riverdale Barracks:

> The object of the manoeuvre is to teach the troops to bivouac and find their own billets, establish headquarters, camps, and put out outposts, just as if they had been landed in a foreign country and had to prepare their own camp, and be ready for inspection if staff officers visited their quarters and also be ready for sudden mobilization to move their forces.
>
> Every unit, including the six infantry battalions, three batteries, Divisional Cyclists, Army Medical Corps and Army Veterinary Corps will be sent out in sections from the camp, and will be expected to reach their allotted areas somewhere in the county by ten o'clock just as if they had disembarked from some troopship and had to prepare camp. After they have established their

Cyclists in ambush.

quarters and lines of communications, all the battalions' artillery and other units will concentrate at the corner of Bathurst Street and Eglinton Avenue and have lunch. They will be inspected and return to camp.[57]

The Cyclists were assigned an area "between Old Mill and Humber Bay on Bloor Street" to set camp.[58]

The first platoons of the 3rd Divisional Cyclist Company set sail for England at the end of November 1915, with the rest catching up at the end of January.

FULL KIT

As with 1st Division Cyclists, 3rd Division Cyclists were assigned to Salisbury Plain (Larkhill Camp). Not much had changed from the previous year: "The whole camp site, with the exception of a few prepared foot paths and roads was nothing but mud. Cycling was practically out of the question and drill on the square impossible."[59] Training was largely limited to "map reading, signalling etc. in the huts."[60]

On February 8, 3rd Division Cyclists moved to Chiseldon Camp where British cyclists and the 2nd Canadian Divisional Cyclist Company were located. Here they were able to get some training in. On March 6, the company did a "heavy test tide thru Savernake forest. Full kit. Raining and hard grind the whole way. Some fainted and rolled over but finished and all in."[61] No doubt there was fainting and rolling over given that full kit was 90 pounds. After another "tough grind" in full kit to "knock the weaklings out" on March 21, "the hut looks like a clothing store, drying out our clothes." [62]

Not all the 3rd Division Cyclists' time at Chiseldon was put to hard training. Shortly after arrival, the "boys" got into a snowball fight with British cyclists who "didn't know how to pack it into snow balls and accused us of putting rocks in our snow balls."[63,64] On March 2, the Cyclists had a "good game of tag on wheels in hut. What a mess."[65] And shortly before departure for the front on March 26, "a number of the men had their hair shaved off leaving only a tuft at front which they waxed in a spike. Said it would be easy for the Germans to scalp them."[66] The 3rd Division Cyclists boarded what one recalled was "a cattle boat"[67] on March 26 for the start of a two-day trip to the front.

4TH CANADIAN DIVISIONAL CYCLIST COMPANY

Recruitment for the ill-fated 4th Canadian Divisional Cyclist Company began February 4, 1916, shortly after the 3rd Division shipped out for England. Like other Canadian Cyclists, "the average age of the men ... was about 20... [they] were from many walks of life but there were very few without high school education coupled with a fair sprinkling having University degrees."[68]

In the depths of winter, training for the 4th Division Cyclists was initially "pretty well confined to route marches, Physical Training and lectures on map reading and military law."[69] With spring, the Cyclists moved outside, going through many of the same drills the 2nd and 3rd Cyclists were put through, including "many Battles of the Humber."[70] Fourth Division Cyclists also participated in some "civic" activities, including

Officers and men, 4th Division Cyclists.

No. 9 Platoon, Cyclists Corps at Exhibition Camp, Toronto.

a Toronto-favourite Sunday bicycle ride known as the Run to High Park. According to the *Globe*:

> A remarkable bicycle run was staged yesterday morning from the South African monument, University Avenue and Queen Street to High Park. Exactly 264 bicyclists participated in the run, including the 109th Cyclist Corps commanded by G.L. MacKay, who headed the procession, and a division of ten lady cyclists. A large

crowd gathered to see the start of the run, before which a batter of motion picture camera men took many feet of pictures. Just before the getaway the 109th Cyclists gave an exhibition of bicycle drill."[71]

The 4th Division Cyclists entrained for Halifax on April 28, 1916, and arrived at Chiseldon on May 6. The Company met its fate shortly thereafter.

5TH CANADIAN DIVISIONAL CYCLIST COMPANY

Enlistment for a 5th Canadian Divisional Cyclist Company began almost immediately after the 4th sailed for England in April 1916. By early summer, platoons from Kingston, Winnipeg, and Vancouver assembled with the Toronto platoons and then moved to Paradise Grove.[72] The fate of the 5th, though, also seemed sealed from the start. According to Cyclist (then-Private) Ken Pettis, "We were called the 'Divisional Cyclist Depot' and had we known what the words meant, that ought to have told us very plainly what was in store. Our ranks were plundered from the very beginning. Several new recruits were drawn into the two senior platoons still at the Exhibition Camp, to go oversees a week after enlistment, with the last of the Fourth Division."[73]

Of the five Cyclist companies created for Canada's contribution to the Great War, the 5th spent the longest time in Canada preparing for war— "nearly nine long months."[74] At Paradise Grove in the summer of 1916, Pettis recalled the company "covered our musketry there and the usual elementary training and at HQ's request made a complete road and billeting survey of the whole Niagara training area.... I am sure we rode thousands of miles and swallowed several tons of dust."[75] In addition to manoeuvres, duties

Personnel of the Cycle Corps and Nursing Sisters leaving Exhibition Camp for overseas service.

included HQ messengers, orderlies, and patrol: "One memorable occasion we patrolled the river road, searching every motor car for Germans who were supposed to be plotting to blow up the International Bridge."[76]

Back at Exhibition Camp in early Fall, "impatiently awaiting word of a move overseas,"[77] Pettis recalled he and his fellow Cyclists "fought the Battle of Humber River a thousand times. We mapped out High Park again and again. There was even a motion-picture filmed of us."[78] At the end of November, the company made a "famous ride" to Hamilton in knee-deep snow along the partially finished highway."[79] The ride was all the more impressive as "the Cyclists made an average speed of 9 ½ miles an hour without casualties."[80]

The 5th shipped out for England in January 1917.

INTERESTING TRAINING, ANYHOW

Overall, the basic training Canadian forces underwent in Canada did not prepare them for the fighting they would face on the Western Front. Nor was it entirely designed to — months of advanced training would take place in camps in England and France prior to moving on to the front.

Lieutenant Baines, Canadian Cyclist Corps, on left. Others unknown.

Francis Royal Brown,
Canadian Cyclists.

In Canada, the countless marches, range practice and other basic drills served rather to "bring this disparate army together. The men marched together, ate together, and slept together."[81] As Pettis reflected, "If our training bore little relationship to the type of warfare then being waged in France, where so-called 'mounted troops' were fighting grimly in the trenches of Sanctuary Wood, it was interesting training anyhow!"[82]

2

The Trenches

The battlefield the 1st Canadian Divisional Cyclist Company and the rest of First Canadian Contingent reached in February 1915 had changed radically since the outbreak of hostilities only six months earlier. In August 1914, the Germans had executed their famous Schlieffen Plan, which involved the bulk of their army smashing through neutral Belgium and invading France from the north and ending up in Paris, while the rest of the invading force would come from the east, thereby encircling French forces. British resistance at Mons, Belgium, and a French-British counterattack at the First Battle of the Marne (the "Miracle of the Marne"), knocked an unsuspecting German force back on its heels, resulting in a stalemate by mid-September 1914. In the so-called Race to the Sea, the two sides pushed north seeking tactical advantage as they dug in defence after defence. Neither was successful. The open warfare upon which the German Schlieffen Plan was built and which characterized the start of the war ground to a halt as both sides literally dug in (see Maps 3 and 4, pages 52–53).[1] Author Tim Cook describes the battlefield the Canadians found themselves on in the winter of 1915 like this:

Trenches were dug deeper; millions of sandbags were stacked above them to provide better protection against snipers' fire and shrapnel bursts; and communication trenches were connected to secondary lines of defence, ultimately to the rear. A vast underground city sprang up along what would become known as the Western Front. In between the two armies was the blasted landscape of No Man's Land, which weaved almost 500 miles from Switzerland to the North Sea, and which would rarely shift east or west during the next four years of war.[2]

On February 17, the Canadians began their orientation to trench warfare under the tutelage of experienced British troops near the French town of Armentières, 30 miles south of Vimy in the Flanders region.[3] But this was not the war — or the warfare — the Cyclists had trained for. Cycling-related duties would in fact be few and far between for Canadian Cyclists for most of the next three years; mostly the Cyclists

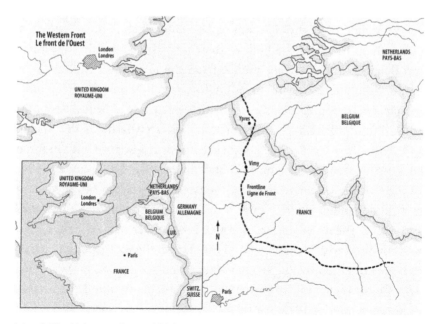

Map 3: The Western Front, 1916.

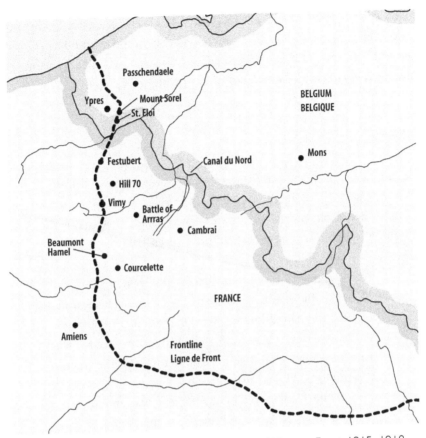

Map 4: The Canadian Expeditionary Corps on the Western Front, 1915–1918.

were assigned "many and varied tasks. These consisted mainly of Traffic Control, Despatch Riding, Mapping and guarding enemy prisoners."[4]

In the trenches near Armentières, 1st Division Cyclists were apprenticed by members of a Scottish battalion. One of their first tasks was "stringing barbed wire in 'No Man's Land'" under the cover of night.[5] The method was effective, if not cumbersome: "first drive wooden stakes into the ground with a large wooden mallet, put a couple of empty sandbags on top of the stakes to deaden the sound a little before stringing the wire."[6] The experience must have been terrifying, with guns flashing in the dark and shells whizzing by their unprotected heads (the distinctive Canadian metal helmets had not yet been issued). The advice proffered by a Scottish sergeant did not help the first Cyclist casualty: "'Don't be afraid, laddies, just stand still when the Verey lights go up and Jerry won't see you.'"[7] In spite of the instructions, one Cyclist was "killed by a sniper, and needless to say, we were glad when the night was over."[8]

YPRES

Beginning April 2, the First Canadian Contingent moved north to the salient west of the Belgian city of Ypres to relieve weary French forces. G.W.L. Nicholson, official historian of the Canadian Army in the First World War, describes the battlefield near Ypres like this:

> At the conclusion of the unsuccessful German attempts to break the deadlock in Flanders in the late autumn of 1914 the Allied line in front of Ypres formed a deep curve seventeen miles long, extending from Steenstraat (on the Yser Canal, five miles northwest of the town) around to St. Eloi (nearly three miles south of Ypres)....
>
> At the focal point of the Salient was the ancient moated town of Ypres, which the Canadians first saw in April 1915. By that time German bombardment had damaged the stately 500-year old Cloth Hall and Cathedral, but many streets were still unharmed, and most of the inhabitants were still living at home. War had not yet devastated the fertile, densely populated area of the Salient. The network of roads which spread out across the Flanders plain linked Ypres with villages, hamlets and farms to north, east and south still tenanted though many were within two miles of the firing line.[9]

On April 22, the relative peace was shattered, first by German bombardments of the front line and Ypres behind, and then, horrifically, by the release of 160 tons of chlorine gas. Luckily, much of the gas eluded the Canadian sector. The French were not so lucky. As one

Cyclist recalled, "Scores of French troops came hurrying from the front line past our billet crying 'the war is finished', the Germans were using poison gas."[10] The French and Algerian retreat created a "yawning gap"[11] on the Canadian's flank which they and the British quickly moved to close as German troops moved forward. The Cyclists "were ordered to 'stand to' ready to move off immediately" for their first engagement in the war.[12]

As Allied forces launched their famous counterattack at Kitcheners' Wood around midnight of April 22, the Cyclists readied for their first engagement of the war as part of an *ad hoc* detachment of Canadian and British reserve battalions. Their mission was to participate in a second counterattack proceeding from the town of Vlamertinge to the west of Ypres west across the Yser Canal below Mauser Ridge. Cyclist Sergeant Frederick Wingfield recalled:

Cyclists (2nd Battalion, Canadian Expeditionary Force) at Scottish lines near Poperinghe, not far from Ypres, Belgium. This photo was taken by an Official War Photographer while the 2nd Battalion was out in rest billets after fighting at Sanctuary Woods, Maple Copse.

That night #1 Platoon under Lieut. Chadwick received orders to proceed to Vlamertinge and cross the canal near that village and proceed until we contacted the Germans, believed to be about two miles north-east of the canal. We arrived at the canal bridge [Brielen] without casualties although the shelling was rather heavy, and met with rifle fire when we attempted to cross the bridge. The Germans had broken through the French lines and reached the canal.

Lieut. Chadwick set up a defence of the bridge and ordered me to take a verbal message back to 1st Div. HQ [at Vlamertinge] and delivered my message to a staff officer. In a few moments I was taken to Gen. Alderson, G.O.C. 1st CDN Div. who asked me to trace on a large wall map the route #1 Platoon had taken, and the bridge we were holding. He then turned to a Staff Officer and ordered him to send re-enforcements to the bridge immediately, then he said to me 'Corporal, you look very tired, go to the barn behind HQ and get a little rest before rejoining your unit, which I think was very considerate of a busy and anxious general.[13]

Canadian forces fought tooth-and-nail over the day, ultimately putting a halt to the initial German advance but at a cost of nearly 1,000 men. The Cyclists were relieved at the bridge mentioned by Wingfield on April 23, having gone without sleep for nearly 48 hours. One Cyclist recalled, "We had to push our bikes along the ditches and I won't forget the gas, tying a wet sock over our mouth and nose helped a little. We had no gas masks or steel helmets in those days."[14] As they moved back to Canadian HQ at Vlamertinge, "the roads clogged with troops pressing forward and refugees trying to get back away from that hell. There were thousands of these refugees moving disconsolately away from their homes as best they could — some with horses and wagons, some with cattle or goats or dogs, carts drawn by tottering old men and women with children in their arms. It was a heartrending site [sic]."[15]

Canadians fought next at the Battle of Festubert, that "pure bloody mess,"[16] from May 15 to June 27 and were involved in minor skirmishes at Givenchy in June and Loos in September. While some Cyclists were "disengaged from the Company and sent on special assignments with other units"[17] during this period, most undertook the "arduous and monotonous" work involved in supporting the logistics of trench warfare — traffic control, dispatch riding, mapping, guarding enemy prisoners, trench guide.[18] Canadian Cyclists would not see significant action again until the Battle of the Somme in the summer of 1916 — and not before a significant reorganization of the ranks.

1ST CANADIAN CORPS CYCLIST BATTALION

In September 1915, the 2nd Canadian Division joined the 1st in France and became the 1st Canadian Army Corps, or simply the Canadian Corps.[19] In March 1916, the 3rd Canadian Division shipped over, with the 4th slated to arrive in August. While most of the regimented units of the divisions remained intact, troop units underwent reorganization. On May 17, 1916, the 1st, 2nd, and 3rd Divisional Cyclist Companies were amalgamated into a single unit called the Canadian Corps Cyclist Battalion, with the former companies "becoming respectively A, B, C Companies."[20] The 4th and 5th Divisional Companies did not survive the reorganization.

THE FAMOUS CYCLIST FUNERAL PROCESSION

While training in and around Toronto may not have exactly prepared Cyclists for battle on the Western Front, it did build esprit-de-corps; 4th Division Cyclists arrived at Chiseldon on May 6, 1916. On June 8, "word came regarding the demise of Divisional Cyclists and the whole out-fit transferred to the 74th Battalion."[21] According to one Cyclist, "Gloom hung over the camp the night before the transfer and everyone talked in hushed tones — now and then there was a burst of righteous indignation, which gave one a new insight into the lives of men who could no longer restrain their pent-up feelings of wrath. Nothing could be done to rescind the order. The transfer must be made the following night."[22] At least the Cyclists were acquainted with the 74th: they had shared quarters with them in the Government Building back at Exhibition Camp in Toronto, although the Cyclists' antics on manoeuvres — the fireworks and other annoyances used to disturb "the Infantry boys … after strenuous days march" and other such "nasty ideas" — were not forgotten by the infantry.[23]

On June 9, 100 of the 199 4th Division Cyclists were sent to Bramshott Camp, where they were transferred to other division units, mostly infantry and machine guns. To help swallow this "bitter pill,"[24] a group of Cyclists gathered to pay last respects to their old Company in the "Famous Cyclist Funeral Procession":

> On the afternoon of the day of the transfer, under a sullen sky, in one corner of Bramshott Camp, a group of sombre, silent lads quietly filed past the "Funeral Bier" of an old Army Cycle…. Two bicycles were used side by side as a hearse and on the cross-bars rested a base, well-covered with someone's blanket, upon which lay the remains of a broken Army Cycle. These remains were draped with a Union Jack together with a large bouquet of wild ferns, cabbage leaves, carrot tops and ragweed. Sixteen [Cyclists] acted as Guard of Honour and, with cape reversed, towed the remains to an old disused trench as the burial place. The procession moved off at 2:30 p.m. led by the muffled drum band of the Unit, followed by a platoon carrying their rifles in a reversed position. Next came the Guard of Honour and Pallbearers followed by the remaining [Cyclists] as official mourners.
>
> Tramp — tramp — tramp in slow march, to the beat of the drums, the procession wound its way through the camp to the open fields and disused trench in the distant horizon. Officers and men of other units stood silently to attention as they passed solemnly by. Presently, the

open grave was reached and the mourners crowded round as the Pall-bearers raised the bier to their shoulders and bare-headed bore the Cycle to its last resting place. Acting padre, Private Savage, with reversed white collar and drooping spectacles, solemnly opened his book and as the dear old Cycle was flung into the trench, sprinkled it with dust of the camp and uttered these now famous words: "Ashes to ashes, dust to dust, if the 74th doesn't bugger us the Kaiser must."

The bugler blew "Last Post" and all the [Cyclists] wended their way slowly back to camp, fully determined to uphold the dignity, spirit and honour of the Cyclists no matter what happened in the future.[25]

The remainder of the Cyclists at Chiseldon were disbanded in July 1916 and similarly transferred to units across the division. Despite having "spent the shortest time together as a unit," 4th Division Cyclists "were outstanding in their service" over the remainder of the war "and there was not a single action undertaken by any Company of the Battalion in which they were not strongly represented."[26]

A similar fate awaited the 5th Divisional Cyclist Company. In late January 1917, the Company left Toronto for Halifax and arrived at Chiseldon in mid-February. At the end of March, the Cyclists were "allotted to one of the three existing companies."[27] As a former member recounted, "our old 'Cyclist Depot' cap-badge could be seen in almost every unit in France; in the infantry, artillery, machine gunners, engineers, pioneer battalions, even in the Railway Troops. In this way we might claim to have 'leavened' the whole Canadian Corps!"[28]

THE SOMME

After fierce fighting at St. Eloi and Mount Sorrel in the spring of 1916, the Canadian Corps moved to the front near the village of Courcelette to fight in the Battle of the Somme at the end of August. The battle had started on July 1, with British forces suffering one of the largest slaughters of the war on that day alone. (It was as part of this offensive, at Beaumont-Hamel, that the Newfoundland Regiment, fighting with the 29th British Division, was almost totally wiped out.) Over the next six weeks, the 1st, 2nd, and 3rd Canadian Divisions fought viciously at Courcelette, Fabeck Graben, Zollern Graben, and Thiepval Ridge before being relieved by the 4th Division in mid-October. These newest recruits inched their way through waist-deep mud and rotting corpses across no man's land, eventually capturing Regina and Desire trenches by the end of the Battle of the Somme on November 19.

Despite their new, unified battalion structure, Canadian Cyclists remained scattered across the Canadian Corps at the Somme, providing largely behind-the-lines support for the offensive, but all "under continuous enemy fire."[29] One Cyclist recalled,

> The Cyclists' work on the Somme consisted largely of carrying ammunition and other supplies, burying cable and other digging parties, with the odd turn at stretcher bearing and burying the dead bodies scattered around all over, many of them half buried already by shell fire. We were not yet doing any actual fighting ourselves but we were in the thick of it most of the time and suffered many casualties. The mud was not too bad for the first few days but soon the whole area turned into a quagmire and made the going very difficult.[30]

In October 1916, Canadian Cyclists were transferred to Vimy Ridge, where they helped prepare for the upcoming battle.

VIMY: "WE WERE TO BE TUNNELLERS"

By the winter of 1916, German forces had retreated to the heavily fortified Hindenburg Line, a 90-mile network of concrete machine-gun nests, barbed wire, communication trenches, and connecting tunnels

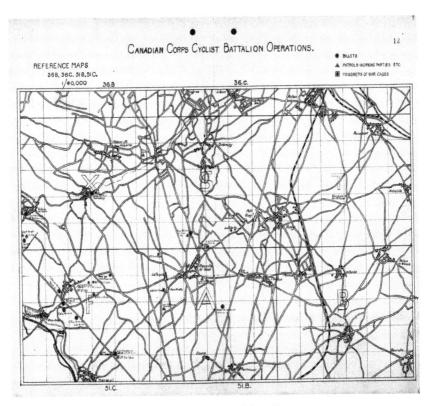

Canadian Corps Cyclist Battalion Operations, Vimy, France.

that stretched from Arras in the north to the Aisne River in the south. At the north end of this line was Vimy Ridge, an escarpment north-west of Arras extending four miles and at its highest peak reaching 65 yards above the Douai Plains. It was one of the highest points along the Western Front — one Cyclist described it as "the finest panoramic view of the war, stretching almost to Douai ten or twelve miles away"[31] — and was the centrepiece of the Hindenburg defence system, serving as a link for German forces in the south to supply lines extending to the Belgian coast on the north.

Central to the Allies' battle plans for 1917 was the capture of Vimy Ridge. Canadian Corps commander General Julien Byng was informed on January 19, 1917, that the Canadians alone would be responsible for this crucial part of the Allies' coming Spring Offensive. To prepare, Byng had the four Canadian divisions stage numerous full-scale rehearsals in a field to the rear of the front. Canadian troops also began to build the massive infrastructure that would move themselves, supplies, light weaponry (245 heavy guns and howitzers would be used in the assault), and over 42,500 tons of ammunition from staging areas in the rear to their positions in no man's land for the final assault.

Byng also oversaw the construction of a network of tunnels to move troops and supplies underground, "one of the great engineering achievements of the war."[32] It is worth quoting G.W.L. Nicholson at length here:

> Tunnelling companies excavated or extended eleven subways of a total length of almost four miles, leading to the Canadian front line. In these electrically lit subways, 25 feet or more underground, telephone cables and water mains found protection from enemy shelling. The subways provided a covered approach for troops moving up for the assault, or in relief, and they allowed a safe and speedy evacuation of the wounded. Chambers cut into their walls housed brigade and battalion headquarters, ammunition stores, and dressing stations; while included in this underground accommodation were several deep caverns, left from chalk-quarrying operations of an earlier day, the largest of which — Zivy cave — had room for an entire battalion.[33]

At Vimy, Canadian Cyclists were assigned to the seven British Royal Engineer tunnelling companies to help build this underground labyrinth. One Cyclist recalled the assignment as "the most slavish and uncongenial work we had during the whole war."[34]

> Towards the end of October [1916] a rumour started that we were to be tunnelers and we started up the line for Newville-St. Vaast via the longest communication trench in the world (Denis La Roque). We then started putting most of Vimy Ridge in sand bags, helping

Imperial Tunnelling Co. dispose of the chalk they dug out of the galleries and tunnels under the German front line, including the famous Grange and Goodman tunnels which were used in the final attack.[35]

The Germans were also busy digging their own tunnels. In this underground theatre, the opposing sides would try to destroy each other's work with artillery and trench mortar fire. Another tactic was to dig a tunnel or mine beneath the opposition's tunnel work, pack it with explosives, and detonate it. Cyclist Private Dick Warren played a role in these underground operations at Vimy. As he recalled:

As each mine had been packed with ammonal and wired, the chamber was sealed and left, till it was time to blow it. These had to be patrolled and I was picked as one of the detail, whose job was to listen and report Fritzy's activities below ground. It was a lonesome and eerie job at times....

Our equipment consisted of Flashlight, Candle and Geophones. The latter were similar to a doctor's stethoscope and had metal containers at one end and were very sensitive, being able to pick up the slightest sound. Armed with these, I entered the "Double Crassiers" tunnel, so named for twin craters on top and which were filled with water. This mine was branched and I took left branch first. I went along the gallery and found it flooded. My candle sputtered out and this warned me of gas, and of course, I did not linger there. I went down the right branch for quite a long way before gas stopped me and so retraced my steps till I found a safe spot. Then, clearing a space on the floor for the Geophones, I sat down and lit a cigarette. With my back against a pit prop and my legs spread wide I placed the plugs in my ears and, hearing Jerry at work I felt at peace in the world. The rats, whose eyes reflected the light from the candle, came so close and no closer and they did not bother me, but their squeaks sounded very loud through the Geophones.

Then a call of nature had to be answered and not wishing to move from my comfortable spot, I proceeded to answer it in the easiest way. A terrific rumble of rushing water sounded in my ears and with the thoughts of the flooded left branch in my mind I figured that I was trapped and had bought it. With my eyes almost popping out and the wind up a mile high, I snatched the plugs from my ears and all was peaceful again.[36]

When the Big Push finally came on April 9, it became evident, at least to the Cyclists, that perhaps "for the first time in the war Germans had lost the upper hand. The roads — or what was left of them — were soon full of German prisoners and walking wounded. One of our jobs here was to check and search the German prisoners before sending them on their way to the rear and within the first few days of the battle we 'processed' over 4,000 of them."[37] The Canadian Corps, with all four divisions fighting side-by-side for the first time in the war, had achieved one of its greatest victories: "The operations had resulted in the capture of more ground, more prisoners and more guns than any previous British offensive on the Western Front."[38]

The trench phase of the Great War would continue for another 16 months after Vimy. The Canadians would fight in two more horrific battles — Hill 70 in August 1917 and Passchendaele (what one Cyclist called "that Hell Hole"[39]) in October and November. Here, as before, Canadian Cyclists were assigned across the Corps to serve in various capacities, such as "traffic control and various working parties."[40] Their role, however, would change radically at Amiens in August 1918.

3

Amiens and the
Full Power of Manoeuvre

The Battle of Amiens (August 8–11, 1918) was a key turning point in the Great War. It came four months after the Germans launched a last, desperate offensive that left their ranks critically depleted (almost 800,000 casualties), supplies spent, and key positions along the Western Front fatally exposed. The Allies, by contrast, fought hard to maintain strategic positions and keep important elements of their force (like the Canadians) in reserve. In addition, by spring, the Americans were sending almost 250,000 fresh troops to the front each month. The tides continued to turn in July with important Allied victories at Hamel and the Marne, and reconnaissance reports showing poor German morale and critical materiel shortages. By July 24, Allied High Command had become convinced the time had come to launch a new offensive, one, in Generalissimo Foch's words, of "such importance as will increase our advantages and leave no respite to the enemy."[1]

As shock troops of the British Empire, proven in major battles like Vimy Ridge, Hill 70, and Passchendaele, the Canadian Corps was assigned to take centre stage in the Allied offensive. The Corps's first assignment was to secure the rail line between Paris and Amiens, a critical link in the

Allied supply chain. Canadian Lieutenant General Currie's three-stage plan for Amiens represented both the culmination of the Corps's technological, tactical advances on the battlefield since 1914[2] (particularly in stages one and two) and a sharp break with how fighting had been conducted (especially in stage three).

Stage one of Currie's plan was a "trench to trench attack" led by the heavy artillery. The gunners would lay down a wall of fire that would creep from enemy outposts to trenches to the rear areas, the so-called Green Objective for the offensive (see Map 2, page 14). While the creeping barrage was not a new tactic by 1918, the Canadians enhanced it by adding machine-gun fire to "thicken" it. The Corps's field guns were also used more surgically in the first stage of fighting to take out enemy gun batteries using reconnaissance from advanced patrols as well as another technological innovation on the battlefield — airplanes.

As artillery fire finished raining down, the second stage of Currie's plan would start — the infantry advance. First would come small groups of advance patrols tasked with sending intelligence back to HQ on enemy positions that survived the initial artillery barrage. The main infantry battalions would then advance and take up those positions, with follow-up battalions "leapfrogging" them and moving the advance forward to the so-called Red Line objective. In this stage, infantry were aided by yet another technological innovation — tanks — whose role was to spearhead through barbed wire and over trenches and provide additional cover to advancing infantry.[3]

With the enemy's defence lines breached, the third stage of battle would begin with mobile forces "sent forward to exploit and seize further ground,"[4] the so-called Blue Line objective.

One of the main architects of the Canadian Corps's mobile warfare doctrine was Brigadier-General Raymond Brutinel. It was his experience and experimentation with mobile warfare earlier in the war that allowed Canadian Cyclists to finally "come into their own" in the Hundred Days campaign, particularly in the open warfare phases of fighting at Amiens, the D-Q Line, Canal du Nord, and the Pursuit from the Sensée Canal.

BRUTINEL AND THE SPRING OFFENSIVE

Born in France in 1882, Raymond Brutinel moved to Edmonton in 1905 and made a fortune in land and oil speculation.[5] It was here that he met Clifford Sifton, the former Liberal cabinet minister in charge of immigration and settlement in the West. The two men shared interests in both business and cutting-edge military technology. At the outbreak of the Great War, Sifton and Brutinel pitched to Minister of Militia and Defence Sam Hughes an idea to organize a mobile motorized machine unit, with rapid-fire machine guns mounted on lightly armoured trucks — the first of its kind in the British Empire. Hughes liked the idea, and in August 1914, created the Automobile Machine Gun Brigade under Major Brutinel, with the Major and Sifton appointed as patrons responsible for purchasing the brigade's first 20 vehicles.[6] In June 1915, the brigade was re-christened the 1st Canadian Motor Machine Gun Brigade (CMMGB).

With fighting done in the trenches for most of the Great War, there was no clear role for mobile units like the 1st CMMGB and it was not readily deployed; Brutinel and his men spent most of their time training and perfecting their use of the machine guns for defensive purposes.[7] The first real opportunity Brutinel had for testing his mobile unit came during the German's Spring Offensive in 1918. Author Tim Cook summarized the 1st CMMGB's role in the offensive like this: "Since the British trench lines had been broken on March 21, the armoured cars now found a role as they raced across the front, providing much-needed firepower and shoring up desperate situations. After driving 150 kilometres north from the Vimy front during the last week of March, the armoured cars covered British withdrawals and punished German spearhead units with raking fire."[8]

On March 22, Brutinel's 1st CMMGB received orders to move from the Canadians' positions at Vimy to support the struggling British 5th Army in its efforts to defend the strongest part of the German advance just east of Amiens. To this end, the 1st CMMGB was organized into five batteries, each with eight machine guns. The first two batteries employed armoured cars, the latter three lighter "box" cars. The brigade was ordered to "hit the gap" (a cavalry term) across the line, support-ing defensive positions, providing cover for British counterattacks, reinforcing infantry lines, "thickening" artillery barrages, and transport-ing ammunition and rations to advanced infantry positions."[9] The 1st CMMGB, as described by one Cyclist, "were moved hither and thither, all up and down the 5th Army front, wherever there was a break-through to be contained, or a gap in the line to be filled."[10] After two weeks of intense fighting, including providing support for Carey's Force at the last line of defence before Amiens on March 30, the 1st CMMGB retired from the line. It had suffered 164 casualties, a rate of more than 40 per-cent of its total complement.[11]

The 1st CMMGB's experience during the Spring Offensive helped Brutinel and the Canadian Corps craft a more comprehensive approach to mobile warfare generally, and the deployment of mobile machine guns specifically. In March 1918, the Corps's machine-gun service was reor-ganized into a single corps battalion under the command and tactical control of a divisional machine-gun commander analogous to the divi-sional artillery commander.[12]

In April, Brutinel and Currie reorganized the motorized machine-gun service as well, adding a 2nd CMMGB to the 1st, each with five 8-gun batteries and eight armoured cars.[13] To support the mobility of the two brigades, a new Canadian Machine Gun Corps Mechanical Transport Company was created to provide administration and maintenance sup-port. Additional "mounted" units would be added to the 1st and 2nd CMMGBs over the course of the Hundred Days campaign as well, including a mobile trench mortar section, a cavalry regiment, a motor-cycle battalion, and the Canadian Corps Cyclist Battalion.

AMIENS, AUGUST 9 — A DASH DOWN THE ROAD

German losses across the Western Front on the first day of fighting at Amiens were staggering: casualties included 650 to 700 officers and between 26,000 and 27,000 other ranks, almost two thirds through sur-render, on August 8 alone. Canadian forces themselves were credited with capturing 5,033 prisoners and 161 guns. German High Command referred to August 8 as "the black day of the German Army in the history of this war."[14] In reporting to the Kaiser on August 10, General Erich Ludendorff said, "We have reached the limits of our capacity. The war must be terminated."[15]

On the first day of fighting, the Canadian Corps had been successful in pushing the Germans back almost eight miles to the old Outer Amiens defence lines. While the Corps had mostly achieved the so-called Blue Line objective for the offensive, one area where they fell short was on the south end of the line at the village of Le Quesnel. Heavy resistance there on August 8 had prevented the 3rd Canadian Division from achieving that portion of its Blue Line objective. The Canadians' first order of business on August 9, therefore, was to capture Le Quesnel and support the French in taking the village of Fresnoy to the south. These tasks fell to Brutinel's Canadian Independent Force (CIF) and elements of the 4th Canadian Division's 75th Canadian Infantry Battalion (CIBn).

At 04:00, 30 minutes in advance of zero hour on August 9, "A" and "B" batteries of the CIF's No. 1 Group, supported by one section of Cyclists from No. 5 Platoon, set off to reconnoitre the roads west of Le Quesnel for the 75th CIBn. At about 04:30, the group "got into action" about 1,000 yards west of the village, ferocious enough to drive it back to HQ. There, the unit joined up with the 75th and were successful in driving German forces out of Le Quesnel at about 05:30, around the same time as French forces captured Fresnoy.

Just after 08:00, the CIF's armoured car detachment set off from HQ down the Amiens–Roye road, along with one section of Cyclists from No. 9 Platoon, to assess the situation between Le Quesnel and Hangest-en-Santerre. The group ran into heavy machine-gun fire from the direction of a wood copse south of Le Quesnel. The Cyclists dismounted and provided cover for the cars to move forward. The cars cleared the woods with an artillery bombardment, "the Gunners on the Cars obtain[ing] excellent targets, killing and wounding many Germans and capturing a few prisoners."[16]

At 09:30, the armoured car detachment and its Cyclists attempted to "make a dash" farther down the road toward the village of Bouchoir.

The "dash" was short-lived — the group ran into heavy shelling and machine-gun fire at a railway crossing just east of the Outer Amiens defence line. A German "whiz-bang" battery supported by machine-gun nests was the main culprit here, spotted by the Cyclists 1,700 yards down the railway embankment. One shell from the 77mm whiz-bang hit one of the cars, killing two men and wounding several others. Cyclist Captain George Scroggie's diary entry for Friday, August 9, includes this commendation for Sergeant Murphy, who was in charge of the Cyclists out with the armoured car detachment that morning:

> Sgt. Murphy, who was in charge of the cyclists sections with the armoured cars at this time showed great coolness in handling his men. He gave clear and concise orders to his men and got them under cover and he bandaged the wounds of one of the men while under heavy machine-gun fire and with the assistance of Pte. Lewarne carried him 500 yards to safety under heavy machine-gun fire. Sgt. Murphy had previously that morning bandaged the wounds of Cpl. Kay and wheeled him to safety down a road swept by machine-gun fire.[17,18]

The armoured car detachment and its Cyclists were relieved just before noon by the CIF No. 2 Group. Continued shelling forced the exhausted detachment and No. 1 Group to retire back to CIF HQ at Maison Blanche.

To support No. 2 Group, the CIF's trench mortar section was brought forward as well. The mortars silenced the whiz-bangs and machine guns with 25 rounds. By this point in the early afternoon, the rest of the Canadian Corps had moved into action, the 5th Canadian Mounted Rifles (CMR) advancing beyond the railroad to the north of the road and the French infantry assisted by their tanks pushing through to the south. No. 2 Group pushed off in the lead: "A" battery advanced to take up positions east of Folies, "B" and "C" batteries moved to Arvillers, where they entered the village ahead of the French. Here, gunner Pte. McCorkell was successful in "capturing 15 prisoners single handed."[19]

General Brutinel's headquarters during the Amiens offensive, looking toward Maison Blanche road and village.

"D" and "E" batteries from No. 2 Group, supported by one platoon of Cyclists, worked their way southeast of Folies and entered Bouchoir with infantry that evening. No. 2 Group took up these positions for the night.

AUGUST 10, 11 — GROUND TO A HALT

Despite the lack of precision that characterized the execution of the battle plan on August 8, the Canadian Corps as a whole was successful in pushing their line another four miles by end of day on August 9. Facing them immediately to the east now were the old trench lines from previous battles — a three-mile-wide belt described by G.W.L. Nicholson as "pitted with shell-holes and befouled with tangles of barbed wire and the remains of old trenches overgrown with long concealing grass marked the position of the former Allied and German front lines before the

German retirement to the Hindenburg Line in the spring of 1917."[20] It was along this line that fighting up and down the Western Front returned briefly on August 10 to its old, familiar trench routine, reinforced by a flood of German troops opposite the Canadians. Eventually, the defensive positions dug into the well-manned trenches effectively ground the Battle of Amiens to a halt the next day, August 11.

Before grinding to a halt, CIF No. 2 Group was engaged in one of the last assaults of the Amiens campaign at Le Quesnoy, a small hamlet 2,000 yards east of Bouchoir. At midnight on August 9, No. 2 Group's transport section lorried the 2nd Canadian Mounted Rifles (CMR) to an assembly area near Bouchoir to ready for the attack. At 04:20 the next morning, under cover from the guns of "A" and "B" batteries located on the Amiens–Roye road, the 2nd CMR entered the village and were successful in clearing it of German forces by 06:30. The batteries, with the support of one section of Cyclists, pushed on down to road and got as far as La Cambuse on the east side of the trenches, but were forced back under heavy shelling. As Canadian forces took up positions along the old

A portion of the Hindenburg Line — a huge mass of barbed wire. Advance east of Arras, October 1918.

British trench from the Battle of the Somme (1916) over the course of the day, No. 2 Group returned to CIF HQ at Maison Blanche. The Canadian Independent Force's role in the first battle of the Hundred Days campaign at Amiens was over.

EXCELLENT RESULTS

At Amiens, the Canadian Corps was ultimately successful in penetrating 14 miles past the Germans' original August 8 positions, liberating 67 square miles of territory and 27 villages, and capturing more than 9,000 prisoners and thousands of guns and ammunition. The victory — "the finest operation of the war," General Byng told Currie shortly after[21] — would be a portent and template of fighting to come over the next 97 days.

Amiens was a particularly significant victory for members of the Canadian Corps Cyclist Battalion. It marked the first time they "finally came into their own. The open warfare gave them a chance to carry out the work for which they were enlisted, namely, as advance patrols and general troubleshooters."[22] Currie noted in his diary on August 15, "I have just finished reading with most intense interest your [Brutinel's] report on Operations conducted by the Independent Force, from the 8th August to the 10th inclusive. In addition to the Special Order which I am publishing, I consider that special praise is due to the Officers and Men of your Command.... I congratulate you most heartily on the success achieved."[23]

Brutinel was more circumspect. While he admitted the "work of the 2 Motor Gun Brigades and the Cyclist Battalion was carried out in a highly credible manner," and their "cooperation with Troops of the other Branches of the service and the French produced excellent results," he believed more could have been achieved. In his words, "Owing to their hasty organization and the little opportunity they had for combined training, perhaps the units did not make full use of the power of manoeuvre, which the addition of Cyclists and Trench Mortars gave them."[24]

In mid-September, Brutinel was successful in getting Currie to make the CIF permanent and begin the preparations needed to realize the "full use of the power of manoeuvre."

4

Arras — A Very Difficult and Tiresome Task

The victory at Amiens convinced Allied High Command that the time had come for an all-out offensive against the Germans. The Canadian Corps received orders to move north 40 miles to Arras on August 22, the 2nd and 3rd Divisions setting off early on August 23, with the 1st and 4th Divisions following over the next five days. The Cyclists themselves set off on the 40-mile ride at 20:00 on August 22 and arrived at Wagonlieu, their old staging area near Arras, at midnight on August 24.

The battlefield the 2nd and 3rd Canadian Divisions faced at the start of fighting on August 26 centred on the Arras–Cambrai road (see Map 5, page 75). Immediately to the east were the old British and German trench systems from the 1917 and spring 1918 offensives. Farther east were additional defensive positions —the Fresnes-Rouvroy Line, two miles in, and then the heavily fortified Drocourt-Quéant (D-Q) Line, located one mile beyond it. The D-Q Line was one of the strongest positions along the Western Front and key to Germany's Hindenburg Line defence. Beyond that was the Canal du Nord, the Canadian Corps's ultimate objective for this phase of the offensive.

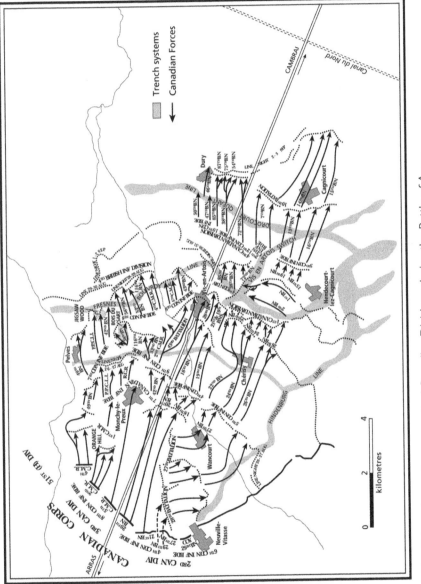

Map 5: Location and movement of Canadian Divisions during the Battle of Arras.

Deployed almost directly off the trains and buses from Amiens, the Canadians literally faced an uphill battle on August 26: Their launching point on the Arras–Cambrai road was near the bottom of the Scarpe and Sensée river valleys, with the hills of Monchy looming 300 feet above and to the east and the 60-foot Orange Hill directly to the north. The 2nd and 3rd Canadian Divisions moved out at 03:00 on August 26 behind their creeping and counter-battery barrages (supported by guns from the 1st CMMGB), driving the Germans out of their trench positions by 11:00.

For the opening phase of the battle, Brutinel's Canadian Independent Force (reconstituted as "Brutinel's Brigade" this time 'round) waited in reserve with orders to be ready to move on four hours' notice.[1]

When the 2nd and 3rd Divisions reported taking the villages of Monchy-le-Preux and Guémappe at 11:00, Currie ordered Brutinel's Brigade to help the 4th Canadian Division relieve the 3rd Division's 7th CIBn from positions on the Scarpe River near Pelves. They ran along

Canadians advancing through a German barrage. Advance east of Arras, September 1918.

the eastern and northern edges of Jigsaw Wood to a sandpit in the south near Boiry. Brutinel's Brigade was instructed to form a defensive flank along the Scarpe River and work to conform the line established by other division elements.

BRUTINEL'S BRIGADE

For the battle at Arras, Brutinel's Brigade was organized into three groups:

- **No. 1 Group** (under the command of Lieutenant-Colonel Lalor) with the 2nd Canadian Motor Machine Gun Brigade with five gun batteries (40 guns), three trench mortar sections, and two Cyclist platoons;
- **No. 2 Group** (Lieutenant-Colonel Chipps) the 101st Machine Gun Battalion with two and a half companies (40 guns) and three trench mortar sections; and
- **No. 3 Group** (Cyclist Major Humphrey) with one machine gun detachment (eight guns), one armoured car detachment (12 guns), and five Cyclist platoons.

On August 27, Lieutenants Scroggie and Goodwill's Cyclist platoons did reconnaissance work on roads in the area. On the evening of August 28, No. 3 Group moved forward along the Arras–Cambrai road and took up positions near the Friction section of the Fresnoy-Rouvroy trench system just west of Pelves. Here the group prepared to advance the next morning.

At 05:00 on August 29, No. 3 Group set out to relieve the 7th CIBn from its positions on the Kit section of the Fresnoy-Rouvroy trench system. The group did so under heavy fire and across a wasteland of shell holes and mud. No. 3 Group was reduced to moving the heavy machine guns one at a time, "shell-hole to shell-hole ... a very difficult and tiresome task." Eventually, the group achieved its objective by 11:00, establishing a line from Boiry to Jigsaw Wood.[2]

Connected by telephone, word arrived back at Brigade HQ that the left flank of No. 1 Group, now located east of Jigsaw Wood, was

Canadian Motor Machine Gun Brigade waiting alongside Arras–Cambrai road.
Advance east of Arras, September 1918.

Scene on the Arras–Cambrai road. Advance east of Arras, September 1918.

exposed. No. 2 Group was ordered forward to help out. As Cyclist Macnab recalled, the Cyclists "left their wheels near Monchy and did a spot of infantry work in the line near the Scarpe River."[3] The attack launched in the early afternoon was led by four Cyclist platoons under Major Humphrey, with artillery support from the 101st Machine Gun Battalion. The Cyclists first took Jigsaw Wood and then Varry Wood, and finally captured the Piccadilly, Regent, and Duke sections of the Fresnoy-Rouvroy trench system "in the face of heavy artillery fire."[4]

All objectives up to and including the Scarpe River were "reached and consolidated" by 17:00. No. 1 and No. 2 Groups dug in to these positions for the night, with the Cyclists and machine gunners set along the river valley facing east and along the Piccadilly and Duke trench sections facing west in defensive position. The groups were relieved by the British 32nd infantry brigade at 07:30 the next morning. At this point, the Cyclists, armoured cars, and trench mortar sections moved into reserve at the Citadel, Arras. The motor-machine-gun brigades remained with the 4th British Division, consolidating and conforming the lines to the east and north of Boiry. These elements of Brutinel's Brigade retired from the line on the evening of August 30.

Canadian Cyclists have a rest.

For the Canadians, the initial phase of the Battle of the Scarpe that dislodged the Germans from the trench system east of Arras ended August 31 with advances of more than five miles and the seizure of most of the Fresnoy-Rouvroy trench system and its 3,300 defenders and various weaponry. For Brutinel's Brigade, "Great credit was due the Commanding Officers for the arrangements and plans of the Operations, and to the Machine Gun Batteries and Cyclists for carrying out the attack, with our Artillery support and in broad daylight, over ground that was being Shelled by the enemy. Our Troops suffered very few casualties and captured about 20 prisoners."[5]

THE D-Q LINE

While fighting continued along the Fresnoy–Rouvroy trench on August 30, Canadian Corps HQ issued orders for the next phase of the battle: the capture of the Drocourt-Quéant (D-Q) Line. The D-Q Line was one of the most well-organized and well-constructed defence systems built by the Germans, replete with concrete shelters and machine-gun nests protected by dense masses of barbed wire. South and a bit west of Dury, the D-Q Line connected to the Buissy Switch, a similarly well-constructed and -defended trench system that connected the D-Q Line with the Hindenburg support system. For G.W.L. Nicholson, one of the most challenging tasks facing the Canadians here was "the necessity of crossing Mont Dury,"[6] located between Dury itself and the Cambrai road: "Advancing infantry [here] would be exposed to fire from machine guns sited on its forward slopes; while covering the crest and rear slope were more guns well-disposed in depth, and farther back the advanced batteries of the German field artillery."[7]

Currie's plan for the D-Q Line assault involved breaking through German lines on a narrow front astride the Arras–Cambrai road, and "swing[ing] onwards rolling up the flanks to the N. and S.," with the 1st Division (British) eventually crossing the D-Q canal and establishing positions on its east bank.[8]

For the initial phase of the assault, the 1st Division would advance on the right of the Canadian line, the 4th Division in the centre astride the Arras–Cambrai road, and the 4th (British) Division under Currie's command on the left. Brutinel's Canadian Independent Force was re-established on August 30 with orders to "push rapidly down the Arras–Cambrai road and attempt to seize crossings over the Canal du Nord" before the enemy blew them up and Canadian engineers had to rebuild them.[9]

THE CANADIAN INDEPENDENT FORCE

For the assault on the D-Q Line, the CIF was organized into five groups, including a new addition to the Force — the Canadian Light Horse regiment:

- Headquarters (under the command of Brigadier-General Brutinel) with 10 motorcyclists, one radio detachment, and one Cyclist platoon;
- Leading Group (Lieutenant-Colonel Whitmore) with one and one half squadrons of the Canadian Light Horse, one section machine guns, six heavy armoured cars, two light armoured cars, and 10 motorcyclists;
- No. 2 Group (Lieutenant-Colonel Walker) with the 1st CMMGB, four light armoured cars, one machine-gun battery, two trench mortar sections, 20 motorcyclists, and the rest of the Canadian Corps Cyclist Battalion;
- No. 3 Group (Lieutenant-Colonel Meurling) with the 2nd CMMGB, one machine-gun section, and 20 motorcyclists;
- Supply Column (Major Arnold) with one water lorry, one fuel and oil lorry, one ammunition lorry, one supply lorry, and five motorcyclists "for Inter-liaisons."[10]

At zero hour, 05:00 on September 2, the Canadian artillery barrage began, with infantry advancing quickly behind the curtain of fire.

Along the Arras–Cambrai road, the 4th Division set off, encountering little resistance until reaching its first objective for the day, on the east side of the D-Q trenches, at around 08:30. Based on intel from reconnaissance reports dropped from a patrol plane,[11] Whitmore's Leading Group set off, "getting in touch with the enemy" around 09:00 east of the intersection with the Villers-lès-Cagnicourt road. Here, the group sent cavalry patrols north to Dury and armoured car patrols southwest to Villers. Neither got very far, both running into heavy artillery and machine-gun fire.

Whitmore's Leading Group was not alone in encountering stiff resistance on the morning of September 2. Up and down the Canadian line, infantry from the 1st, 4th, and 4th British Divisions were delayed by Germans dug deep into their positions. In Brutinel's words,

> Several Batteries of German Field Artillery and Trench Mortars were firing over open Sights from the high ground between Saudemont and Buissy. The Village of Villers-lez-Cagnicourt [sic] had been fortified by the enemy by placing Machine Guns and "Minewerfers" in the houses. The Factory on the Cambrai Road, N. of the Village, and the Sunken Villers–Saudemont Road were strongly held by the enemy and proved formidable obstacles. Even after capture later in the day, the enemy Gunners still commanded all the approaches from the W. to all these positions.[12]

To give 4th Canadian Division forces an extra push, Walker's No. 2 Group was sent forward. First, its "E" gun battery supported by two Cyclist platoons passed through the 32nd CIBn and set off down the Arras–Cambrai road: "15 mins after this party left and proceeded over crest of hill. They were subjected to heavy artillery and MG fire from direct observation and Capt. Brosseau was wounded. Lieut. Sellers was killed along with numbers of others. This party was too badly cut up to proceed on their mission but took up positions in trenches and shell holes on sides of road."[13]

The gunners and Cyclists remained at this position for the day, "engaging many good targets" despite heavy fatigue.[14] Next, "D" battery and two more Cyclist platoons leapfrogged "E" battery and established themselves at a concentration of buildings along the road north of the village of Villers, but were held 500 yards short by machine gun and artillery fire from their left flank. Two light armoured cars then set out for the Villers-lès-Cagnicourt–Saudemont intersection, but had to return and get two Cyclist platoons to help clear a blockade formed by fallen trees. Finally, "A" battery and two more Cyclist platoons moved into position behind "D" and "E" batteries. By late afternoon, No. 2 Group had three gun batteries and six Cyclist platoons in position on both sides of the road between Dury and Villers. But as the afternoon "wore away, it became evident that an organized Infantry attack on both sides of the Area occupied by the Canadian Independent Force would be necessary to overcome the enemy resistance."[15] Near midnight, No. 2 Group was relieved by the 11th and 12th CIBns and the entire CIF withdrew from the line.

Transport driver with a load of captured machine guns and trench mortars. Advance east of Arras, September 1918.

12th Brigade Signal headquarters, Dury. Advance east of Arras, September 1918.

Scene at a Canadian YMCA tent. Advance east of Arras.

A DEGREE OF PERMANENCY REQUIRED

For all intents and purposes, the Canadian offensive on the D-Q Line ended late on the night of September 2, when German forces pulled back on a wide front to positions along the eastern side of the Canal du Nord. By noon the next day, the entire Canadian Corps moved in general advance across the open fields to the west bank of the canal. Reconnaissance units reported all bridges across the canal destroyed and the east bank strongly held. Allied and German forces drew to a stalemate once again, with Allies dug in along the west side of the canal, the Germans on the east, both sides taking time to rest and reorganize for the next stage of the offensive. The Canadians had earned a well-deserved break after what Currie called "one of the finest performances in all the war."[16]

Once again, Brutinel was more circumspect. In his notes on the D-Q assault, Brutinel judged that his force had ultimately failed to accomplish its mission of securing the bridgeheads on the Canal du Nord at Marquion. The problem, he assessed, was not a lack of firepower or any imbalance in organization needed to overcome the enemy forces. Rather, he argued, the force's firepower had not been "properly wielded" due to having been "hastily put together at the last minute." To resolve this, Brutinel recommended to Currie that his mobile force be established with a "degree of permanency" rather than the "spasmodic extemporizations" that characterized its composition to date. Permanency, Brutinel argued, would allow the troops to train together and "learn their possibilities and limitations, acquire mutual confidence and unity of purpose ... confidence in the support that they will receive promptly, unselfishness and devotion to duty, based on a broad and comprehensive Esprit de Corps."[17]

Brutinel was persuasive: on September 19, Currie ordered that Brutinel's Brigade be established on a permanent basis, just in time to begin preparations for the assault on the Canal du Nord.

5

Canal du Nord — Sticky Fighting

On September 3, Allied Generalissimo Ferdinand Foch outlined the next phase of the offensive: an audacious assault along the entire front, with Belgian forces in the north aimed at Ghent and Bruges, British forces aimed at Cambrai and St. Quentin, the French in the centre aimed toward Aisne, and the Americans beginning at Saint-Mihiel and aiming toward Mézier.[1] This offensive would not be the "lethargic blows" that had characterized the battles of 1915–17, but in Foch's words would be the "subtle crippling punches of a skilled boxer, elusive and wary, but crowding his opponent towards defeat."[2]

For this next phase of the Hundred Days campaign, the Canadian Corps was assigned to take the Canal du Nord. G.W.L. Nicholson describes the Canadian positions here:

> A mile south-east of Dury, at the highest point where the Drocourt-Quéant system crossed the Arras–Cambrai road, stands the Canadian Memorial to the soldiers who broke through that famous defence line. In the centre of a small park surrounded by holly hedge and maple trees a simple square block of stone

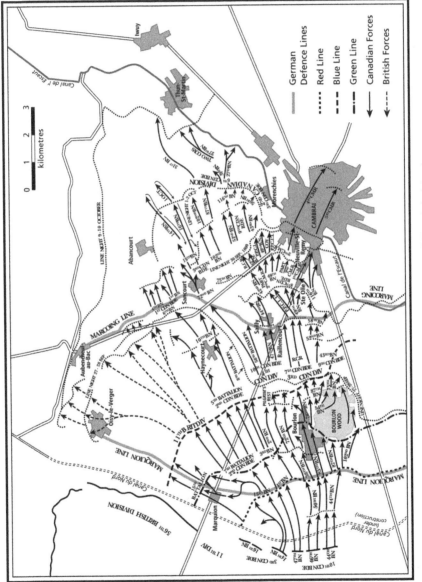

Map 6: Canadian positions and movements during the Battle of Canal du Nord.

carries the inscription beginning, "The Canadian Corps 100,000 strong." From its base one looks westward toward Arras over the terrain so gallantly captured by the Canadian divisions. To the south-east lie other battlefields. Seven miles away, to the right of the straight road reaching down to Cambrai, the observer can discern on a clear day the high mound of Bourlon Wood silhouetted against the sky. To the Canadians dug in on the Dury ridge in September 1918, this was a significant landmark, for they knew that between the wood and themselves lay the next major barrier in their path — the Canal du Nord.[3]

The Canal du Nord itself was a north–south, 60-mile-long waterway linking the Canal de la Sensée at Arleux with the Canal Latéral à l'Oise near Noyon. Construction on the canal had begun in 1908, but the outbreak of the war had left it only partially constructed. It was basically a trench between 40 and 60 yards across, the western bank reaching about 10–12 feet high, the eastern four or five feet high. To the east and north of

The famous Canal du Nord showing construction and cutting, across which Canadians crossed with their supports and supplies. Advance east of Arras.

Another view of the Canal du Nord.

the canal, the Germans had flooded the surrounding marshlands, adding to their natural defensive position. The section of the canal immediately in front of the Canadians was also partially flooded. All of this was well-covered by enemy machine-gun positions on higher grounds to the east — especially at Bourlon Wood — with well-dug-in defensive lines located in Marquion and Marcoing trenches systems between the canal and the key German logistics hub located at the city of Cambrai.

BRUTINEL'S BRIGADE REDUX

Overcoming the Canal du Nord and achieving the subsequent objectives required a detailed, well-thought-through battle plan and considerable training that would combine all elements of Canadian Corps forces — artillery, infantry, tanks, engineering, supply — in a way not previously deployed.[4] Currie's audacious plan was to cross the canal at an un-flooded section south of their main position at Dury in a narrow, 2,600-yard defile, then rush forward and fan out along a front initially 9,700 yards wide to one 15,000 yards, move forward on the right to seize Bourlon Wood, and then on the left to take the canals at l'Escaut and Sensée east of Cambrai (see Map 6, page 87). Currie's ultimate goal was to help the British and French take Cambrai itself.[5]

Cambrai was central to German logistics in the Flanders theatre, the lynchpin in the Hindenburg defence line. For military historian Shane Schreiber, Currie's plan for the Canal du Nord and objectives around Cambrai would become his "operational masterpiece, the culmination of his education as a general."[6]

At the canal, a key feature of Currie's battle plan was once again the deployment of mobile troops, especially when the conditions for open warfare arose. On September 19, Currie acted on Brutinel's recommendations and established "Brutinel's Brigade" as a permanent unit "directly under the Order of Corps Headquarters."[7] This iteration of the force, which would exist until the end of the war, was composed of the 1st and 2nd CMMGBs, the Canadian Light Horse regiment, the Canadian Corps Cyclist Battalion, and at least one battery of field artillery and one trench mortar section "whenever the situation permits."[8]

For the assault on the Canal du Nord, Brutinel's Brigade was instructed to prepare for a variety of tasks, including "thickening up" machine-gun barrages, seizing "tactical features in advance of our Line and holding them until the arrival of the Infantry," participating in the Corps's general advance, and serving as rearguard — whatever was "required by the situation."[9] To prepare for the assignment and build the "broad and comprehensive Esprit de Corps" he thought the force lacked at Amiens and Arras, Brutinel and his team developed a specialized two-week training program, which he described like this:

> All the NCOs and Gunners went through a short course on the Vickers Gun, and were lectured by their Officers on the Duties of all Members of a Gun Crew, on Indirect Fire, Barrage Fire, the value of Cover, the necessity of close cooperation with the other Batteries and all Arms of the Service, and on other Allied Subjects. Batteries did individual Tactical Exercises as a preliminary to Exercises in

cooperation with other Batteries. Exercises were carried out in which a number of Dismounted Batteries assisted with Direct and Indirect Fire a Mounted Battery whose advance had been held up: Batteries received Training in advancing in pairs and in mutual assistance against Defended Localities and Strong Points. Many Tactical Schemes were executed in which a group of Motor Batteries, a few Platoons of Cyclists, a Detachment of Armoured Cars, and a number of Motor Cyclists took part. All the Schemes and Exercises were followed by discussions and criticisms with a view to emphasizing special points and drawing lessons for the future.[10]

The tactical exercises were supplemented by a variety of sports, both traditional ("indoor baseball and football") and non-traditional ("Guard Mounting, Revolver Shooting, getting into Action wearing a Small Box Respirator").[11] Competition was reported as "keen," leaving the ranks in "high spirits" and "quite ready to join in the next hunt of the Canadian Corps."[12]

For the assault itself, Brutinel's Brigade was to be held in reserve until the Marcoing Line was taken. It was then to advance forward to secure the bridges over the Canal de l'Escaut between Cambrai and the Canal de la Sensée to the north and east. The actual place of engagement and specific method of organization were not spelled out, left to be determined "largely on the success of our Infantry and on the nature of the Roads and the resistance encountered."[13]

THE NEXT HUNT

The Canadian offensive on the Canal du Nord began on September 27 with an artillery barrage at 05:29. Over 320,000 rounds were fired by 640 guns across the Canadian line, including those from the 1st and 2nd CMMGBs. Behind this barrage, the canal itself was quickly taken, as was the Marquoin trench. Advances by 4th Division fighters on the right

The Hundred Days Offensive, August–November 1918, Battle of the Canal du Nord. Canadian Infantry Regiment waiting in the Canal du Nord to go forward. Near Moeuvres, September 27, 1918.

The Hundred Days Offensive, August–November 1918, Battle of the Canal du Nord. Infantry supports going forward, 4th Canadian Division, September 27, 1918.

moved with relative speed to the village of Bourlon and then on to Bourlon Wood. Here the Corps encountered some of the most intense fighting of the war as troops moved tree-to-tree clearing out German machine gunners and infantry. On the left of the Canadian line, 1st Division units advanced almost 10,000 yards to the Marcoing Line on their first push.

On the evening of September 27, scouts from Brutinel's Brigade reported that the "opportunity for a break-through" was not likely to happen — the village of Raillencourt on Arras–Cambrai road at the Marcoing Line was still in enemy hands.[14] The brigade remained at the ready through the night. This would become a familiar pattern for the next four days.

On the 28th, the 1st, 3rd, and 4th Canadian Divisions resumed their ferocious attack. Based on reconnaissance received throughout the day, Brutinel's Brigade moved to various jumping-off positions ready to advance. At 09:00, all units moved from Sains-lès-Marquion to a wind-mill on the Sains-lès-Marquion–Bourlon road. From here, they moved to Maison Neuve. Throughout the afternoon, brigade patrols kept in touch with units all along the Canadian front, but "no action developed."[15] The 3rd Division got held up north of Fontaine-Notre-Dame and the 4th near Sailly.

On the 29th, the brigade received reports that 4th Division infantry had advanced past the railway north of Sancourt. The brigade readied again — the Canadian Light Horse moved west of Sancourt, the 2nd CMMGB and two armoured cars moved up the road through Sailly, the 1st CMMGB and two armoured cars were dispatched down the main Cambrai road, and the Cyclists took up positions north of Sailly ready to support the CLH "in any action that might develop."[16] Once again, none did, owing to the lack of progress by advance forces.

On the 30th, the brigade moved forward once again, "ready to push forward at a moment's notice."[17] Acting as patrols, Cyclists and cavalry kept in touch with forward units all day, but again no opportunity to advance presented as the fighting ground down: "The progress of our Infantry was very slow. The enemy, who had thrown into the battle oppo-site the Canadian Corps 3 or 4 fresh Divisions, offered a very determined resistance. The fighting became 'sticky.' No favourable opportunity for employment of Mobile Forces occurred. The Cavalry, Motor Brigades, and Cyclists were therefore ordered back to the same positions they had occupied on the previous night."[18]

Despite the "sticky" fighting and mounting casualties, the 1st and 4th Divisions achieved their objectives — gaining five miles on September 28 alone — but then stalled into a series of deadly attacks by the Canadians and counterattacks by the desperate Germans. On both September 28 and 29, Canadian casualties were more than 2,000 each day, with another 1,000 on Sunday the 30th. By the end of the five days of fighting, 13,620 Canadians had been killed, wounded, or taken prisoner. On October 1, Currie called a halt to "the deadly cycle of diminishing returns,"[19] having captured more than 7,000 prisoners and 205 guns, overtaken the three defensive systems to the west of Cambrai, and secured strategic jumping-off points for the next phase of the battle. Little new development occurred between October 2 and 8 in the Canadian sector. On October 2, Brutinel's Brigade joined the 2nd Canadian Division and 11th British Division in helping to "maintain and consolidate positions gained … [and] reorganize in depth." The Canadian Corps and Brutinel's Brigade would not see widespread action until the Battle of Cambrai the next week.

6

Cambrai — Take Advantage of Any Opening

The Canadians were not the only ones battered but successful in recent fighting. Up and down the Western Front, British, French, Belgian, and newly-arrived Americans had shattered German defensive positions from Verdun to the sea. These, and other Axis losses, prompted Germany to seek an armistice with the Americans on October 4. As discussions began, Allied forces pressed on.

When fighting halted on October 2, Canadians were positioned to the north and west of Cambrai, the British to the south. Allied orders on October 6 were to carry out a two-phase operation: the British 3rd Army was to advance and capture a strategic ridge immediately to the southeast of Cambrai. Then, the Canadians were to advance over the Canal de l'Escaut between Morenchies and Ramillies and establish positions with the British behind Escaudoeuvres. The manoeuvre was designed to envelop Cambrai and force the remaining Germans therein to surrender. Brutinel's Brigade was placed on standby once again, with instructions to be ready to secure the bridges along the Canal de l'Escaut northeast of Cambrai and generally "take advantage of any opening to exploit success."[1] As with the Canal du Nord phase of the operation, the "actual

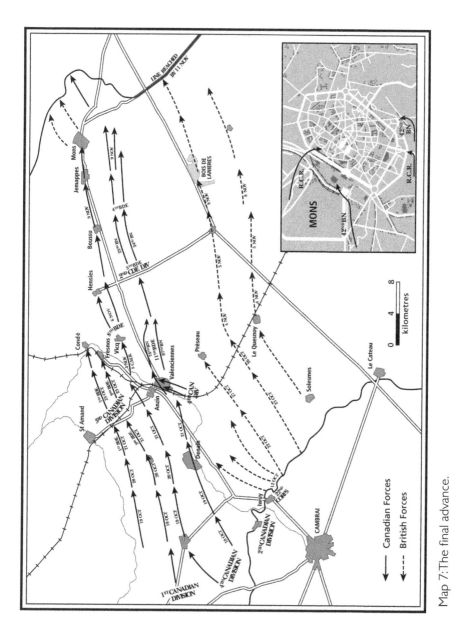

Map 7: The final advance.

Canadians entering the square in Cambrai, France, with three sides of the square on fire. Advance east of Arras, October 1918.

place and method of engagement and the composition of the Groups of the Brigade were not definitely laid down. Its Operation would depend largely on the initial success of the Infantry and on the nature of the Roads and the resistance encountered."[2]

OCTOBER 9

Zero hour for the attack on Cambrai came at 01:30 on October 9, with a four-and-a-half-hour artillery barrage. At 08:30, infantry began their advance and quickly discovered there was little resistance: air reconnaissance confirmed German forces were in retreat to positions beyond the Selle River, part of the heavily fortified Hermann Line, Germany's last before the German border (see Map 7, page 96).[3] As the 3rd Canadian Division prepared to enter Cambrai, the 2nd Canadian Division moved northeast beyond the city along the Canal de l'Escaut with orders to clear the area between the canals of enemy positions and provide cover for the Third Army's left flank.[4] The situation presented "one of the rare occasions when it seemed that mobile forces might be profitably employed."[5]

Of all the elements of Brutinel's Brigade, the Canadian Light Horse (CLH) detachment saw the most work on October 9. Early that morning, Brutinel received word from 2nd Canadian Division HQ that infantry were making good progress pushing past the canal and ordered the Canadian Light Horse to be ready to "seize, as soon as the opportunity

The lock gates and bridge, Canal de l'Escaut, mined by the Germans when driven from Cambrai by the Canadians. November 1918.

Canadian engineers bridging Canal de l'Escaut on Arras–Cambrai road. November 1918.

arose, the high ground between Naves and Thun-Saint-Martin as a first bound, and the high ground E. of Iwuy-Rieux Road, as a second bound."[6]

The CLH moved into jump-off positions southeast of Morenchies on the west of the canal. By 10:00, reports came in that the 25th CIBn had entered Escaudoeuvres, the 6th CIBn was in Eswars, and the 11th British Division had pushed through into Thun-l'Évêque. "B" Squadron CLH set off along the Cambrai–Iwuy road, getting as far as the railway before encountering enemy machine-gun fire and "men and horses were seen to fall."[7] Under heavy fire, the main body of the troop "dashed forward" and took up positions on the high ground between the railway and a road east of le Marais, where they dug in with Hotchkiss machine guns.

From its commanding position on the high ground between Thun-Saint-Martin and Naves, the main body of "B" Squadron and its Hotchkiss guns provided cover for one CLH troop to try to outflank German positions by crossing the railway east of Escaudoeuvres, splitting up into attacking parties and galloping northward as far as the railway running to Naves. Here the troop ran into barbed wire and machine guns, forcing them to dismount and dig in. At the same time, a second troop worked its way along the left flank between Thun-Saint-Martin and Iwuy, but it, too, was forced to dismount and dig defensive positions when it ran into well-organized machine-gun nests and "well-directed rifle fire."[8] The CLH held these positions throughout the afternoon in the face of increasingly aggressive artillery fire.

By 18:00, the CLH had advanced to an average depth of 2,000 yards on a front of about 2,000 yards. At this point the CLH was relieved by two platoons of Cyclists drawn from "A" and "B" Companies.[9] The advance had been costly: 12 horses were killed and 25 wounded on October 9. The rest of the brigade suffered a dozen human casualties, including Cyclist Private Bill Mennill, who was injured as he moved into position with his platoon: "While firing up this road in a criss-cross manner, I was the target of a machine gun burst, and retired from active duty back around a bend in the road."[10]

The rest of Brutinel's Brigade spent October 9 manoeuvring behind the 2nd Canadian Division waiting for an "opening to exploit success." At 08:00, the brigade (minus the CLH) was put on notice it would "move off immediately."[11] At 10:50, it moved to Escadoeuvres and crossed the Canal de l'Escaut on the Pont D'Aire Bridge and set up HQ. There, at 17:00, reports came in that 2nd Division infantry had attacked again, trying to seize the ground between Naves and Thun-Saint-Martin. Brutinel ordered the 1st CMMGB, four armoured cars, and four Cyclist platoons from "C" Company to work up the Cambrai–Naves road, cross the Erclin River, and seize the high ground east of the Iwuy–Rieux road. The detachment returned at 21:00 having found the 3rd Division infantry attack held up by heavy machine-gun fire from the railway embankment west of Naves and the British on the right driven back near Cagnoncles. Here the brigade dug in for the night.

OCTOBER 10 — POOR OLD JAKE

Brutinel's trench mortars launched the offensive early on the morning of October 10 by firing 25 rounds on a nest of 10 enemy machine guns located along the railway about 1,000 yards west of Naves. By zero hour (06:00), the mortars had silenced the guns and the rest of the brigade went to work.

First off the line that morning was a detachment of four armoured cars and four platoons of Cyclists. As soon as news came that infantry had captured Naves at around 09:00, the cars and Cyclists set off down Cambrai–Saulzoir road and seized the bridgehead across the Erclin River, the first of the previous day's objectives. At this point, the crews dismounted and "dashed forward" with guns and took up positions astride the Naves–Saulzoir road 1,200 yards east of the river, where they "received a great deal of attention from the enemy Machine Guns situated on the high ground N. of the Main Road and from a Party of Germans holding the Sunken Road just in front of our Machine Gunners and Cyclists."[12] The sunken road was soon cleared by four guns from the 1st CMMGB and three additional platoons of Cyclists who had moved forward in support.

Meanwhile, as the armoured car detachment set out on the morning of October 10, Brigade HQ also sent out Canadian Light Horse and Cyclist patrols to assess crossings over the Erclin River north of the

Cambrai–Saulzoir road. The patrols found all bridges in the vicinity destroyed, but noted a small stretch of the riverbed just north of Naves–Villers-en-Cauchies road was dry. As reports came in that the infantry advance was going well, "A" Squadron and two troops of "C" Squadron CLH crossed at this point and rode north — straight into enemy rifle and machine-gun fire, with "A" Squadron losing practically all their horses. Cyclist Bill Mennill saw the slaughter from his position with the 2nd CMMGB to the right of the squadron's rush:

> We were in the centre of a rolling wooded plain, to the north-east and to our left and right were low lying hills. Soon things began to happen. Over the ridge to our left came a troop of the Canadian Light Horse at full gallop. This did not turn out to be a particularly successful manoeuvre as the German Machine guns opened up on them, the horses rearing, plunging and dying. They were soon halted....
>
> It was apparent that this plain was very well covered by enemy machine guns, and that some of them were stationed directly in front of us. We opened up with the Vickers and Lewis guns, firing up the road, and our other men with rifles and grenades.[13]

"C" Squadron, along with dismounted "A" Squadron riders, pushed on "with great determination" until they reached a cut bank near a set of buildings on the side of the Rieux–Iwuy road. Here, terrific gunfire cut down most of the horses of "C" Squadron.

Once word got back to Brigade HQ that the CLH could no longer advance, the 2nd CMMGB and two Cyclist platoons were ordered forward to provide relief. "B" Battery and half of "D" Battery along with the Cyclists went forward, while "A" Battery and the rest of "D" were deployed immediately to the west. Under cover provided by "A" guns, "B" Battery and the Cyclists got as far as the sunken road 1,200 yards east of the Erclin where they met up with the armoured car detachment. Cyclist Macnab was with this group and described their advance like this:

As No. 5 Platoon coasted down the long grade toward Naves, Fritz, who had us under direct observation from his high ground, stepped up his artillery fire on the village and by the time we started through it the main street was a shambles of shell holes, bricks, telephone poles and wire and "coal boxes" were bursting in all directions. It was a case of riding through "hell for leather and the devil take the hindmost." To the best of my knowledge we got through Naves without casualties, though "Jake" Jacobs was forcibly dismounted when some telephone wire became entangled in the pedals of his "gas pie charger."[14]

Macnab continued with details of the advance — and the fate of "poor old Jake":

Clearing Naves, we continued down the road until stopped by the blown and wrecked bridge over the Erclin River, about 1 ½ miles from the village. Here we left our cycles beside the road and continued on foot, fording the river which was shallow at this point. Fritz had evidently kept good track of us and now cracked down salvoes of "Grass cutters," that type of shell which burst on immediate contact, without digging a crater. We all took to the roadside ditch, with the exception of "Jake" who had now caught up to us. He crouched behind a brick wall where he was a "sitting duck" for the flying shrapnel. Several of us yelled at him to get away from there and into the ditch where he could have cover. He ran for it, but, as he dropped into the ditch beside me, another salvo burst around us and a chunk of shrapnel punctured his helmet and lodged in the crown of his hood. His rifle, which in his excitement he had left leaning against the wall, was demolished by the same shell burst. Jake claimed that he felt no pain and would not believe that he was wounded until I showed him blood from the back of his neck. After slapping a shell dressing on his head, I told him to try to work his way to the rear as best he could.

In the meantime, two Motor Machine Gun trucks had come up from Naves to the wrecked bridge. Unable to cross the river they were frantically gee-hawing around trying to get turned in the narrow road in order to get the hell out of there. Fritz now lifted his fire from us and went after the trucks and we immediately started working our way up the road once more. We heard later that Jake caught a ride on one of the MG trucks, but was killed when Fritz scored a direct hit on the vehicle. Poor old Jake — it just wasn't his day — as we used to say, "his number had come up."[15]

Eventually the 2nd CMMGB and No. 5 Cyclist Platoon found the crews from the armoured car detachment and its Cyclists. Under cover provided by the combined guns of the "A" and "B" Batteries, those of the armoured cars and the CLH troops, two Cyclist platoons were sent out on advance patrol. One proceeded parallel to the Naves–Saulzoir road, which succeeded in dislodging the enemy machine gunners and infantry from the high ground 1,000 yards east of the sunken road. The other platoon suffered a number of casualties as they attempted to advance but were forced back. Cyclist Macnab was with this group:

> We now found that the "C" Co'y platoon, in trying to get forward, had suffered a considerable number of casual-ties, about one third of their strength. They were holding the sunken road, from the point where it joined the main road to a point about 500 feet north, where it turned sharply to the left. Any attempt to get around the corner was met by a hail of machine-gun fire from a well con-cealed hun, manned by a "Fritzie" who fired at the least excuse. Likewise any attempt to get forward, by climbing out of this rather deep sunken road (the sides were from

10 to 20 feet high), received the same attention from this and other guns. In other words, we were pinned down, for the time being, so sat tight until dusk.[16]

Brigade forces dug in here, with the CLH and Cyclists handing over their positions to the troops from the 19th and 20th CIBns later that evening.[17] As they moved back across the Erclin, Cyclist Macnab suffered one last insult:

> We were not ready to think of getting forward again, but were relieved by the 19th Battalion. They came up from the rear in extended formation and took over the sunken road while we wended our weary way back to the river crossing. Here we found that many of our cycles and our packs had been riddled with shrap from the shell fire. That is where I said goodbye to my trusty old Planet Junior Cycle, which had been issued to me in the Spring of 1915 in Toronto and which I had babied and scrounged parts for up to that point. It was cut in two and my pack was full of shrap.[18]

Early on the morning of October 11, British forces resumed the advance on the brigade's right. Guns from the 1st CMMGB provided cover from their positions achieved the previous night. By early afternoon, fighting had once again ground to a halt: the German line along the east side of the Sensée would remain in place here — and farther north opposite Iwuy — for another day. On the afternoon of October 11, the remainder of Brutinel's Brigade were withdrawn and replaced by British forces.

FINE SPIRIT OF COMRADESHIP AND CO-OPERATION

Capturing the Canal du Nord and Cambrai is remembered as some of the most complex and difficult fighting conducted by the Canadian Corps — "the finest example of its professionalism in the Great War"[19] according to historian Jack Granatstein, Currie's "operational masterpiece, the culmination of his education as a general"[20] for Schreiber. Aside from the technical challenge posed by crossing the canal itself, the Canadians had met and defeated 12 German divisions supported by 13 machine-gun companies.[21] This added to the Canadians' overall record of achievement since the Hundred Days campaign had begun two months earlier. As G.W.L. Nicholson described:

> In 47 days the Corps had fought forward 23 miles against very strong resistance. The opposing forces had been identified as belonging to as many as 31 German divisions, though many of these formations were already badly depleted. Under Currie's firm direction the Corps had functioned well and smoothly; its casualties were many, but by First World War standards not excessive in the light of their task. The total officially reported killed, wounded and missing between 22 August and 11 October numbered 1,544 officers and 29,262 other ranks. In achieving its victory the Corps had captured 18,585 prisoners, together with 371 guns and nearly 2,000 machine guns. Besides depriving the enemy of the great distributing centre of Cambrai, the Canadians had liberated 54 towns and villages standing on more than 116 square miles of French soil.[22]

The Canadians' success owed to a number of factors: the rest and training it had prior to August 8, the large reserve created with the broken-up 5th Division, excellent leadership, a new and innovative battle plan, a significant record of success in the field, and a strong esprit de corps. As Granatstein put it, "Canadian division commanders knew each other and their men, they were accustomed to working together because they had trained and fought together from the outset, and their Corps leadership knew how to get the best from them."[23] Brutinel observed the emergence of a similar esprit de corps in his brigade at the Canal du Nord and Cambrai: "The repeated attempts of the Canadian

Light Horse to push forward against heavy enemy Fire, and their determination to hold the ground they had captured ... was a noteworthy performance. The Work of the 2nd C.M.M.G.B. and the Cyclists ... was most noticeable, not only in the way in which the Units were handled and all Ranks tried to fulfill their various duties, but in their fine spirit of comradeship and co-operation."[24]

The permanency Brutinel had sought for his brigade and was granted in September had paid off. The brigade's "fine spirit of comradeship and co-operation" would continue to inform operations during the Pursuit from the Sensée Canal, arguably the Canadian Cyclists "most telling work."[25]

7

Pursuit from the Sensée — Their "Most Telling Work"

By the time they withdrew from the line on October 11, the Canadians were exhausted. Since August 8, the Corps had advanced 23 hard miles through a landscape scarred by the trenches and barbed wire of old battles and new defensive lines, conquering difficult geography filled with canals, muddy marshes, and dense woods, all the while engaged in vicious, bloody fighting with 31 German army divisions. Over this period, the Canadians suffered almost 43,000 casualties. The period of rest, reorganization, refitting, overhauling, training, and sports[1] over the ensuing five days was not, in Nicholson's words, "unwelcome."[2] Allied forces in general were ordered to keep close touch with the enemy over this period, but actual fighting was to be limited to patrolling, raiding, and test barrages used to confirm enemy positions.[3]

The situation changed dramatically on October 17. Early-morning test barrages failed to draw the usual retaliation indicating enemy positions (see Maps 7 and 8, pages 96 and 109). Patrols were sent out to investigate; their reconnaissance confirmed the Germans were indeed in full retreat up and down the line.[4] German High Command, in fact, had ordered forces to pull back on October 15 and regroup behind the shorter and less vulnerable Hermann Line anchored at Valenciennes, eight miles to the north and east with a view to "possibly re-start[ing] Trench Warfare."[5] The German plan, however, required time to deploy, which they hoped to buy with a "well-planned system of demolition" that "destroyed the Railways, blew up the Bridges and Road junctions, laid Mines at frequent intervals in the Main Road, flooded the Canals, and fought skillful Rearguard action with specially well-trained Machine Gun Detachments."[6]

Beginning October 17, the Allies aimed to interrupt this "well-planned system of demolition" by maintaining constant contact with the retreating forces and, to hasten the retreat, generally "annoying him as much as possible."[7] Schreiber describes the open warfare doctrine employed in the Pursuit like this:

> … the forward divisions advanced with one brigade forward, where possible, leapfrogging the brigades as they became exhausted. The brigades followed suit, pushing forward a new battalion roughly every day. The infantry were usually preceded by a forward screen of cavalry, cyclists and armored cars, as well as trench mortars and some field artillery detachments, whose job it was to maintain contact with the enemy rear guard, and push them aside if possible. The ground captured by the armored cars would then be occupied by the infantry, and the gains consolidated.[8]

To provide this "forward screen," Brutinel's Brigade was deployed across the Canadian divisions as follows:

1st Division:
- "B" Squadron, Canadian Light Horse
- "A" Company, Canadian Corps Cyclist Battalion
- "C" Battery, 1st CMMGB
- "E" Battery, 1st CMMGB
- 2 Armoured Cars

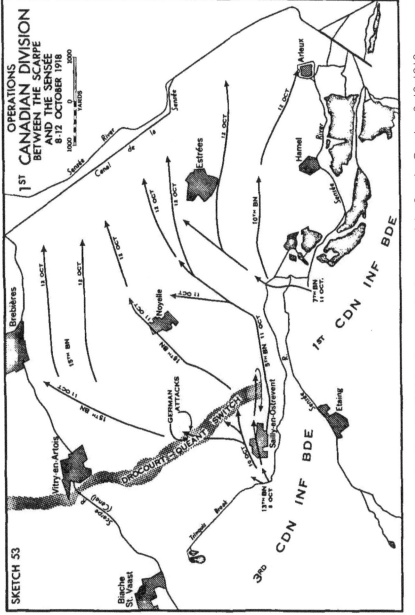

Map 8: Operations, 1st Canadian Division, between the Scarpe and the Sensée, October 8–12, 1918.

2nd Division:
- "B" Company, Canadian Corps Cyclist Battalion

4th Division:
- "C" Squadron, Canadian Light Horse
- "C" Company, Canadian Corps Cyclist Battalion
- "C" Battery, 2nd CMMGB
- "E" Battery, 2nd CMMGB
- 2 Armoured Cars

In general, the mobile units of Brutinel's Brigade were tasked with providing reconnaissance patrols for the attacking divisions. The units were to "keep in constant touch with the enemy as it retreated and communicate enemy positions and anything else of importance like road and bridge status to the infantry coming behind."[9] Cyclists and cavalry troops also provided runners to keep Brigade HQ connected as they advanced over the open territory.[10] Cyclist Macnab described the Cyclists' work from October 17–23 like this:

> The Independent Force was now organized as pursuit troops operating with the Cavalry, mounted 6" howitzers and engineers and getting in perhaps their most telling work. They cleared out many village and machine-gun nests in advance of the infantry and protected the engineers when the latter constructed or repaired the bridges across canals or streams. They also tested the roads and villages for mines and "booby" traps….
>
> Being out in advance most of the time we never knew when we were going to run into trouble and lost quite a few men killed and wounded. Sometimes it would be snipers; sometimes machine guns; sometimes field artillery using "open sights," that is, firing directly at us from positions in the open. During this stage some of our men were attached directly to various battalions for advance guard duties.[11]

PURSUIT

On the morning of October 17, the Canadians held an almost 20-mile front with the 1st Division holding positions on the left of the line. At zero hour, the 1st Division moved across the Canal de la Sensée and pushed rapidly northeastward, moving through the abandoned villages of Dechy, Roucourt, and Douai and well beyond the Douai–Cambrai road by evening. The 4th Canadian Division, in the middle of the line, and the 2nd Division, on a much smaller front on the right, encountered much heavier resistance along their sectors of the canal and were not able to cross until well after midnight on bridges built by the engineers at Pont Rade.

Brutinel's troops got into action on the morning of October 18. Working with the 1st Division, 3rd Troop of "B" Squadron CLH and No. 2 Cyclist Platoon from "A" Company reported to 102th CIBn HQ, where they received orders to "gain contact with the enemy and keep the Battalion constantly informed of the situation."[12] Four patrols were organized (two cavalry, two Cyclist) and set out from Quenesson Farm

Canadians advancing through swamps of River Sensée, 200 yards from Rémy.

northeast of Bugnicourt along the Monchecourt–Écaillon road. The patrols found enemy troops just north of Monchecourt and reported the information back to 102th CIBn HQ. Cyclists with No. 1 platoon were used as "runners" to keep battalion headquarters "in touch with the Companies in the Line and the Units on the Flanks."[13] Cyclists with No. 3 Platoon were organized into a patrol and sent toward Lewarde to make contact with the enemy. These Cyclists attracted machine-gun fire on the southern outskirts of Auberchicourt.

With the 4th Division in the middle of the line, Cyclists from No. 7 platoon "C" Company were organized into two patrol parties, one reporting to the 46th CIBn and the other to the 50th CIBn. The first party set out at 08:00 for the village of Marq, where it encountered heavy machine-gun fire. The 46th advanced to this position, where it spent the night. The second patrol set off with one CLH troop in the direction of Émerchicourt, where it, too, ran into heavy fire from guns along the Auberchicourt–Monchecourt road. They returned to 50th CIBn HQ at Monchecourt for the night.[14] Cyclists with No. 8 Platoon were assigned to work with the 3rd Troop CLH as patrols for the 11th CIBn with orders to "gain contact with the enemy and to keep the Battalion constantly informed of the situation."[15] At 08:00, they set off organized into four patrol parties — two cavalry, two Cyclist — encountering enemy positions north of Monchecourt and along the Monchecourt–Écaillon road.

The pursuit continued on the morning of October 19. With the 4th Division on the right, 3rd Troop CLH and No. 8 Cyclist Platoon were organized into four patrols and sent off at noon through Abscon. Their orders were to move east of the village and maintain the position until the 11th CIBn caught up. The CLH patrols then set off over open ground, the Cyclists along the roads. The CLH reached Bellevue and Haveluy, reporting both clear of the enemy. By evening, the Cyclists made it to Fosse Lambrecht and le Chauffour.

Cyclists with No. 7 Platoon set off in advance of the 46th CIBn through Mastaing and Roeulx and then into Denain by 13:30 on October 19. Here they found "9 Germans who retired hastily as soon as they saw our Men."[16] Once the town was cleared of enemy forces, Cyclist Macnab recalled being "nearly mobbed" by grateful civilians.[17] This would become a recurring theme for the Canadians as they liberated over 70,000 civilians in 52 towns and villages before reaching Valenciennes on November 1.[18] Moving to the eastern outskirts of Denain, the No. 7 Cyclist Platoon encountered enemy machine-gun fire and held the position until the advanced guard of the 44th CIBn arrived. From there, these Cyclists were assigned patrol duty in advance of that battalion.

The 1st Canadian Division continued to sweep through its sector on October 19. With the division now in full flight, "A" Company Cyclists and most of the CLH worked as runners and small advanced patrols to ensure consistent movement and straight lines. Overall, the Canadians made great progress on October 19: by day's end they had moved their front almost 12,000 yards, the longest single-day advance the Canadians made during the Great War.[19] The advance also narrowed the Canadian front, effectively "pinching out" the 2nd Division and sending it into reserve.

For Brutinel's troops, October 20 began with No. 3 Cyclist Platoon working in advance of the 1st Division (14th infantry battalion) and encountering stiff resistance from machine-gun and artillery fire first at Wallers, the last town before the Forêt de Vicoigne, and then just south of the forest. The Cyclists were successful in flushing the nests out and holding the positions until the 14th CIBn arrived. No. 1 Cyclist Platoon got as far as the Goulee Station on the southwest side of the Forêt de Vicoigne. By dusk, the 1st Division had established a line extending along the western and southern edges of the forest. On the right with the 4th Division, No. 7 Cyclist Platoon traded their bicycles at 05:00 for a small rowboat and crossed the Canal de l'Escaut south of Denain, where they made a reconnaissance of Bouchy. The village turned out to be deserted. No. 9 Cyclist Platoon caught up with No. 7 there about 09:00 and organized into four patrols with the task of gaining and maintaining contact with the enemy east of Denain. The Cyclists were successful, "coming under heavy M.G. fire but located many enemy M.G.s and snipers ... and reported position to Infantry and Trench mortars."[20] On reconnaissance in the area, "E" Battery and one armoured car tried to assist, but could not proceed beyond Wallers as the main inter-section had been destroyed. Working in advance of the 54th CIBn, No. 8 Cyclist Platoon set out at 08:30 from Escaudain to Bellevue and Haveluy, rousting out machine-gun and sniper nests along the way.[21]

October 21 was a relatively quiet day. On the left of the Canadian line, a motorcycle patrol reported to 1st Canadian Division HQ that the roads and bridges along the Aniche–Abscon road south of Fosse Fénelon had been blown up. Most of the tired 1st Division's efforts that day were spent working with the engineers to rebuild bridges and fill craters. One group of Cyclists did some patrol work — No. 1 platoon worked its way into the Forêt de Vicoigne as far as the Saint-Amand–Valenciennes road, where the enemy was temporarily established. The Germans withdrew in the evening and the 3rd Canadian Division came forward to relieve the 1st.[22] This would be the last time the old First Canadian Contingent would see action in the war.[23]

On the right, a CLH patrol advanced as far as Rouvignies for the 44th CIBn and to Château de Malplaquet for the 87th CIBn. Working in advance of the 44th and 47th CIBns, Nos. 7 and 9 Cyclist Platoons set out at 04:00 and proceeded through Rouvignies to Prouvy, where they met up with a third Cyclist party. From here they proceeded northward along the main road to Valenciennes until they were pinned down by a field gun just south and west of the town. The 44th CIBn deployed to this position and waited for the rest of the division to arrive.

Patrol duty continued for the Cyclists on October 22. Cyclists from No. 1 Platoon were transferred to the 3rd Division's 9th CIBn where they "furnished leading patrol which located M.G.s at crossroads Etoile de Cernay."[24] Cyclists with No. 2 Platoon (attached to the 42nd CIBn) organized into two patrols to conduct reconnaissance in the western portion of the Forêt de Raismes. In advance of the 52nd CIBn, No. 3 Cyclist Platoon also set off and met enemy cavalry about one mile south and east and an enemy patrol on a road to the north. Both enemy parties retreated upon contact. Cyclist Macnab described the encounter like this: "The Germans had their cavalry out but they were not much opposition. For example, the day after passing through Denain some of our Cyclists bumped into one of their patrols in a heavy fog. They were already mounted and did not wait to say good-bye but took off at a gallop, stopping only long enough as they passed a 'whiz-bang' gun behind them to start the gun shelling us."[25]

Macnab's patrol party established contact with 4th Division troops later on the southwest edge of the forest. Overall, based on the intel provided by the gunners, CLH patrols and Cyclists, 3rd Division forces were able to advance through the forest inside of 15 hours and establish a position 7,000 yards from their start point.

Over on the right side of the shrinking Canadian line, Cyclists and CLH detachments with the 4th Division were also kept busy with patrol duty. CLH patrols moved through Anzin, Marivaux, and Beuvrages by the end of the day in advance of the 11th CIBn on the division's left flank. In the middle of the division, Nos. 7 and 9 Cyclist Platoons worked in advance of the 85th CIBn and the 78th CIBn on the main road, No. 8 getting by machine-gun fire and snipers while advancing toward la Sentinelle, No.7 making it to Saint-Waast-la-Haut by evening. The 2nd CMMGB and the armoured cars used their guns to protect the division's right flank, particularly in the afternoon along the Anzin–Bruay road, where "enemy Machine Guns had inflicted many casualties on the Crews."[26] In working to clear the road, Corporal Anthony, one of the armoured car drivers, "greatly distinguished himself when the steering rod of his Armoured Car had been broken, he walked along in front of the Car, under heavy Machine-gun fire and steered it by hand into a place of safety."[27]

October 23 was the last day of the Pursuit from the Sensée. With the refreshed 3rd Canadian Division on the left, "C" Company Cyclists were used as dispatch riders and runners between infantry units as they

A Canadian Cyclist shouting down a dugout in German for men to come out. Advance east of Arras.

settled into positions along the Canal de l'Escaut and as patrols to reconnoitre roads for infantry and artillery movement. Cyclists with the 4th Division served similar functions on the right as it settled in into position. By end-of-day, the Canadian portion of the front extended eight miles south and west along the canal from the village of Fresnes, north and east of Valenciennes, to the extent of the northern flank of British forces at the village of Odomez on the south. All elements of Brutinel's Brigade were withdrawn from the line on October 24. The Canadian Corps would spend the following week preparing for the assault on Valenciennes, Brutinel's Brigade in particular taking "advantage of a comparatively quiet interval to rest and refit and also to overhaul their Transport and Equipment. A little General Training was done every day; and sports and concerts helped to fill in the days Programs."[28]

THE UTMOST GALLANTRY AND VIGOUR

The almost 30-mile pursuit of the retreating Germans from the Canal de la Sensée Canal to the Canal de l'Escaut from October 17 to 23 represented some of the Canadian Cyclists' "most telling" work. For the Canadians in general, it was one of the few times during the Great War that they were in full motion, experiencing almost as much of a challenge keeping supply lines and artillery connected to the quickly advancing forces as engaging German rearguard actions. And the key to the advance was the success of Brutinel's force, which worked at the bleeding edge of the push. In an open letter to the Canadian Corps, Major-General Sir David Watson (commander of the 4th Canadian Division) expressed his "appreciation of the valuable assistance rendered us by the Units at our disposal by the Corps during these last few days' operations." In Watson's words,

> I refer particularly to the work of the Squadrons of Cavalry, the Cyclists and the Armoured Cars and affiliated Guns in Lorries with Crews. From first to last, these Units have cooperated with our Infantry with the utmost gallantry and vigour. They have carried out the

orders and work allotted to them with the greatest satisfaction. Time and again Armoured Cars have been sent around to help in outflanking Machine Gun positions. On certain occasions these Armoured Cars have been sent out with Parties of Engineers, dropping these at various points where Roads required mending, and then coming back for additional loads. The Cavalry, acting as Patrols, have kept us constantly in touch with the enemy, carrying out this hazardous work with great skill and complete satisfaction; while the Cyclists have been most valuable in their excellent Patrol duties as well as carrying Dispatches and securing information regarding enemy movements and positions of our own Troops.

From both Brigades in the Line, I have the same excellent reports of the work of these Units, and I am anxious that they should receive the full credit for the splendid results they have given me.[29]

8

Valenciennes and Mons

The assault on Cambrai was to be the Canadian Corps's introduction to urban warfare in the Great War. German desertion of the city on the eve of the Canadians' assault on October 9, however, made the Battle of Valenciennes on November 1–2 the Canadians' first urban engagement (see Map 7, page 96).

Valenciennes was the last major French city still held by the Germans on October 30, and it stood as a key obstacle to the Allied advance along the Western Front. It was heavily fortified, anchoring the last major German defence system, the Hermann Line. Geography aided the German defences here as well. To the south, the Germans had fortified positions on Mount Houy, a 160-yard-high wooded highland that commanded the l'Escaut Valley to the south of Valenciennes. On the west and north sides of the city, the Canal de l'Escaut combined with the German trench system running alongside formed a second key barrier to attack. Five divisions of the German army were dug in to these positions. On the morning of November 1, Canadian forces faced off directly from the south.

Across a front of 2,500 yards, Currie's plan of attack on Valenciennes was for the 4th Canadian Division to dislodge the Germans from their defensive positions atop Mount Houy with a massive artillery barrage early on the morning of November 1. Then, after the 3rd Division had crossed the Canal de l'Escaut on the left of the Canadian line, infantry units would advance on Valenciennes itself, moving street by street, house by house, "mopping up" the city. (The Allies had forbidden Currie

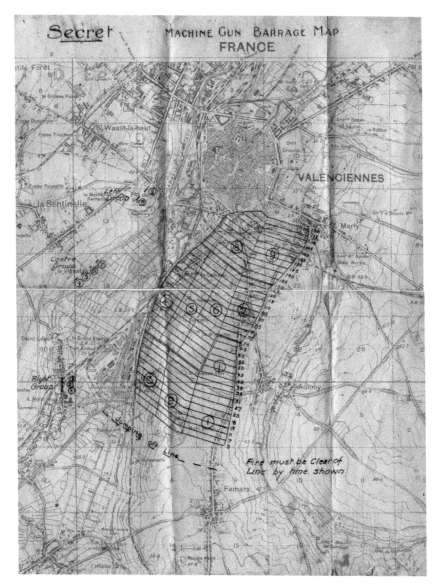

Mount Houy barrage map.

from using artillery within the city due to the large French civilian population.) The Canadians also had a deadline: the main Allied advance on Germany was to resume November 3.

Zero hour at Valenciennes came at 05:15 on November 1, with one of the largest artillery barrages unleashed in the war, the magnitude of which warrants quoting G.W.L. Nicholson in full:

> Because its left wing, on the west side of the Escaut Canal, had advanced so far forward, the Canadian Corps was able to arrange a rather unique artillery barrage on the Mont Houy position. Eight field and six heavy artillery brigades supported the 10th Infantry Brigade in its attack. Three field brigades sited south of the Escaut, near Maing, supplied the frontal creeping barrage; one gave oblique fire from the left bank near Trith St. Leger; the other two were near La Sentinelle, west of the Cambrai–Valenciennes road, furnishing enfilade fire along the enemy's flank. Unable through lack of suitable bridges to cross the Escaut, the heavy artillery remained on the left bank in a position to bring oblique, enfilade and even reverse fire (deliberately arranged for moral effect) on the area of the attack. Some three and a half brigades were employed, on counter-battery work, the remainder bringing down fire on houses which were suspected of containing machine-gun nests. Three batteries of 4.5-inch howitzers fired an intense smoke-screen to cover the attack, and the normal artillery barrage was supplemented by the fire of twelve batteries of the 1st and 4th Canadian Machine Gun Battalions firing in close support or in enfilade from north of the canal. On no other occasion in the whole war was a single infantry brigade to be supported with such a weight of gunfire.[1]

As per Currie's plan, 4th Division infantry advanced after the initial barrage and took Mount Houy by 06:00. The 3rd Division was equally successful on the Canadians' left flank, crossing the Canal de l'Escaut and pushing north of Valenciennes by mid-morning. Elements of the 4th Division advanced the remaining mile and a half to Valenciennes itself, with the 44th and 46th infantry brigades crossing the canal and entering the city in the early afternoon.

At Valenciennes, three units from Brutinel's Brigade were assigned to the 4th Division — the 1st CMMGB, one Canadian Light Horse squadron, and one company of Canadian Corps Cyclist Battalion ("B" Company). On the morning of November 1, the 1st CMMGB was assigned to the 4th Division MG Commander to help support the hurricane barrage.[2] The bulk of CLH and Cyclist troops were employed as dispatch riders and runners "between Headquarters of Brigades and the advanced Battalion Headquarters and also for keeping up Communication between the Scouts, Patrols, Companies and Infantry Report Centres."[3] The remainder of Brutinel's force was assigned patrol and reconnaissance duties, sending reports back to HQ on the disposition and positions of 4th Division troops, enemy strength and location, and the state of critical infrastructure like bridges and roads. Cyclist Macnab described "B" Company Cyclists' assignment at Valenciennes like this:

> By October 31st advance parties had reached the Canal de l'Escaut, where it passes through the outskirts of Valenciennes. Here all the bridges had been blown up but next morning (November 1st) some Cyclists [working on the left flank of the 10th CIBn] got across on a canal lock gate and established a bridgehead. The Germans had set fire to the buildings along the canal and between fire, smoke and snipers, our lads had quite a hot time until the engineers got over and stopped the fires.
>
> The Cyclists then proceeded on through Valenciennes, clearing out snipers and machine-gun nests. They were officially recorded as the first British troops to go through the town. Three of them, however, never came out as they were killed in action — the

victims of enemy machine-gun fire. Here as in other cities and towns the civilians were very helpful in clearing out Germans hiding in houses.[4]

Vastly outnumbered and dangerously under-strength, the 10th and 12th infantry brigades pushed through the streets of Valenciennes from west to east using reconnaissance reports from two patrols from "B" Company Cyclists working in advance. Just before 09:00, the Cyclists reported back to brigade HQ that "the town was clear of the enemy."[5]

The 10th and 12th brigades "joined hands" on the eastern outskirts of the city north of Marly shortly after 09:00. From here, one armoured car with one Cyclist patrol set off toward Saint-Saulve on the Valenciennes–Mons road and got to a cemetery northeast of Marly where they took up positions against enemy machine guns. "D" Battery guns advanced to these positions and waited for infantry from 54th CIBn to relieve them around noon. The car set off on its own

Canadians going into Valenciennes over an improvised bridge, November 1918.

toward Mons in the early afternoon, getting as far as a slag heap on the southeast side of the village.

Against the odds, "those at the sharp end" of the Canadian advance through Valenciennes "cleared the enemy positions, one at a time, in countless stand-up battles that went largely unrecorded in the official records."[6] Currie made this entry to his diary at the end of fighting on November 2: "The operation yesterday was one of the most successful the Corps has yet performed."[7] A small part of this success was due to Canadian Cyclists, which the commander of the 72nd infantry battalion noted in his report: "The work of the Cyclists attached to this Battalion throughout the recent Operations cannot be too highly spoken of and their services in reconnoitring Cross-roads and Tactical Points was of immense value. The reports rendered to Battalion Headquarters during the operations were concise and accurate."[8]

ACT VIGOROUSLY

The capture of Valenciennes was the last set-piece battle the Canadian Corps fought in the Great War. Although the Canadians and the rest of the Allies were preparing for another on November 3, early-morning reconnaissance confirmed the Germans were again in retreat. Allied HQ ordered a general advance, with individual divisions instructed to "act vigorously" on their own initiative and keep the Germans from establishing firm positions.[9] Units from Brutinel's Brigade, still attached to the 4th Division after Valenciennes, continued to be deployed as patrols and other capacities as needed. On November 2, two squadrons of CLH and three platoons of Cyclists were used as dispatch riders, runners, and orderlies between the various brigade and battalion headquarters "and also for keeping up Communications between the Scouts, Patrols, Companies and Infantry Report Centres."[10] One battery of guns from the 1st CMMGB ("E" Battery) and one platoon of Cyclists from "B" Company were sent out as patrols in advance of division infantry once again. Cyclist Macnab described the final push from Valenciennes to Mons like this: "German opposition was slackening but there was still quite a bit of heavy fighting along the Valenciennes–Mons road — unfortunately right up to November 11th."[11] This type of engagement would repeat itself day after day over the ensuing week.

Working on a much narrower front from the Valenciennes–Mons road on the north to Préseau on the south, 4th Canadian Division forces pushed forward almost to the Estreux–Onnaing road on November 3 without much resistance from the enemy; 3rd Division forces to the north made similar progress. Resistance from the topography was another story. The countryside east of Valenciennes and into Belgium had many more villages, deeper valleys and rivers, and densely treed expanses than encountered up to that point. The roads themselves were made largely impassable by large shell craters, encountered especially at key crossroads. What roads did exist, and the work-around detours hastily built by the engineers, were used by artillery and the lorries from ever-lengthening supply chains. Adding to the chaos were the autumn rains — only one day from November 1 to the 11 was without heavy precipitation. For Brutinel's mobile forces — especially the Cyclists — this all added up to limited deployment on the final push. On November 3rd, for example, one of the armoured cars and a platoon of Cyclists could only make it halfway from Marly to Estreux "Owing to Mine Craters N. and E. of the Crossroads the Roads were impassable and prevented the Armoured Car from reaching its objective."[12]

At 05:15 of November 4, "E" Battery from the 1st CMMGB and No. 6 Cyclist Platoon were ordered forward to keep in touch with the enemy and "harass his retreat."[13] The roads, however, delayed the gunners, so the Cyclists "pushed on alone to Onnaing, where an enemy cyclist patrol was met and a Lewis Gun post established. About 20 of the enemy were encountered here. The post was relieved at 10:30 hours by the 72nd CIBn."[14] Little resistance was encountered as the Canadians moved through town, save for a few retreating enemy patrols. At the eastern exit of town, though, much stronger resistance was encountered by "E" Battery, which had caught up to the action. The gunners let loose with their eight guns, "forcing the enemy to abandon his positions."[15] The Cyclists, meanwhile, advanced on the north side of the main road, capturing a few prisoners along with their two field guns.

Upon establishing their line on the east of Onnaing, the Cyclists and gunners found the Valenciennes–Mons road from Onnaing to Quarouble destroyed by mines and made impassable to mobile units. As they set up their positions and waited for infantry relief, stiff enemy fire was encountered; the gunners moved through a cemetery on the right of the cratered road, the Cyclists on the left along the railway. By early afternoon, the enemy guns were out of action.

On the morning of November 5, the 72nd CIBn caught up and established a line connecting the Cyclists and gunners and began organizing the next stage of the advance on Quarouble. Engineers were summoned forward to fill the craters and begin making the road passable for motor vehicles. At 09:00, though, enemy resistance heated up again, artillery first taking out one of the CMMGB's armoured cars and then laying down enfilade fire on the Canadians' new positions, "greatly annoying our own Gun Detachments."[16] The CMMGB, the Cyclists, and the 72nd CIBn fought for position throughout the day, eventually establishing a line about 600 yards to the east of Onnaing.

The 12th CIBn had much more luck to the south of Onnaing. By the early morning of November 5, infantry took the next town along the road, Quarouble, and engaged in heavy fighting over the course of that day and the next. By the evening of November 6, 4th Division forces had established a line along the sunken road immediately to the east of Quiévrechain. The 4th Division was then relieved by the 2nd Division and retired from the line for the last time in the war.

Meanwhile, on the left of the Canadian line, the 3rd Division worked its way east on the north side of the Valenciennes–Mons road, now heavily flooded as a result of Germans opening sluice gates on the canal, as well as the heavy autumn rains. The 3rd Division also encountered pockets of vicious resistance, first at the mining town of Vicq from November 4 to 6, and then at Condé alongside British forces from November 7 and 8.

FINAL PUSH

On November 7, the Canadian Corps crossed into Belgium. On the right, the 2nd Division had orders to "act with the utmost boldness" on the final push to Mons.[17] To aid in this last act, Brutinel's Brigade was reorganized into a two-detachment Independent Force. The Southern Detachment included two squadrons of Canadian Light Horse, two batteries of gunners from the 2nd CMMGB, and one subsection of engineers; the Northern Detachment consisted of two gun batteries, one subsection of engineers, and "B" Company of the Canadian Corps Cyclist Battalion under the command of Captain Scroggie.[18] The Independent Force had orders to "advance through the Infantry and work ahead of them" if the enemy's line of resistance was broken or its rearguard pierced." While the infantry of the 2nd Division made excellent progress over the next four days, the almost complete demolition of the roads effectively grounded the Independent Forces' mobile units during this period.

On November 7, the Force moved out from Rombies and Quarouble, but immediately came to a halt: the road had been destroyed by four mine craters 40 feet in diameter and 12 feet deep. Independent Force troops dismounted and worked with the engineers for six "hard and continuous" hours to fill and bridge the craters. Around noon, the troops remounted and set off down the Valenciennes–Mons road, only to be stopped again at 16:00 by another huge mine crater 1,000 yards east of Quiévrain. The Force retired for the evening, leaving the engineers to source additional bridging material.

A similar routine was followed on November 8: 2nd Division infantry made good progress, reaching the Dour-Hainin Line by noon, but the wheeled units of the Independent Force were sidelined again by systematic mining of the roads and the nonstop rain. Not needing the roads to navigate, the two CLH squadrons were redeployed to the 4th and 5th CIBns as contact patrols and dispatch riders for the duration of the war.

On November 9, the Canadian Corps was on the move once again. To the north, 3rd Division forces were closing in on Mons, the Patricias reaching the suburb of Jemappes that evening. To the south, after much bridging, the Independent Force managed to get to Frameries, three miles southeast of Mons by the evening of November 9, where it reported to 6th CIBn HQ.

On the morning of the 10th, the Independent Force moved to the intersection of the railway and the Maubeuge–Mons road and helped infantry overcome a spirited point of resistance at the Bois la Haut, a wooded hill rising 350 feet above the countryside 2,000 yards to the southeast of Mons. Once at the intersection, the North Detachment headed north, but quickly ran into artillery and machine-gun fire. Here, enemy resistance held out until 03:15.[19] The South Detachment under Captain Scroggie did not fare much better, its progress arrested just north of Ciply by a blown-up bridge. Engineers estimated it would take the better part of the remainder of the day for the bridge to be repaired, so Brutinel's force retired to Frameries for the night.

By the evening of November 10, the Canadian line ran west from Saint-Symphorien, where the 2nd Division had advanced to, around the south and western outskirts of Mons to Nimy, where the 3rd Division was centred.

Mined crossroads just outside Mons, Belgium, November 1918.

11TH HOUR — DID NOT KNOW THE WAR WAS OVER

The attack on Mons began at 23:00 on November 10 with 3rd Division infantry advancing from the east, south, and north ends of the city. By daybreak, the last of the remaining Germans (who had begun their retreat around midnight) had been pushed out. It was around this time, 06:30 on November 11, that Canadian Corps HQ received a message from Allied High Command that hostilities were to cease at 11:00 that morning. As it took some time for word to reach all units, the pursuit of the retreating Germans continued that morning, with 3rd Division infantry pushing to a point almost five miles east of Mons and Brutinel's troops with the 2nd Division pushing from the south.

Early on November 11, the Independent Force set out from Frameries ahead of the 6th CIBn through the suburb of Spiennes to the southeast of Mons. The "very bad state of the roads," however, prevented the Force from "gaining touch" with the retreating enemy, save for one armoured car in the village of St. Antoine by 10:30. Major Humphrey from the "C" Company Cyclist described the last advance made by Canadian Cyclists in the Great War on November 11 like this:

> Company left Frameries at 06:30 hours and moved to Spiennes to co-operate with the 2nd CMMGB — the latter were unable to get as far as Spiennes owing to roads being blown. At 10:00 hours Canadians received word that hostilities would cease at 11:00 hours and a message was received by the Company to withdraw to Frameries. The company came under heavy shell fire from 10:45 hours to 11:00 hours, but fortunately no one was hit. Company passed the day and night in Frameries.

Cyclist Macnab recalled how the end of the war ended for members of "B" Company of the Canadian Corps Cyclist Battalion: "On November 11th there was naturally a big celebration in Mons, including a march past, but some of our men who were then over three miles past Mons did not know that the war was actually over at 11 o'clock until a German official car came through to arrange the take-over by the British."[20]

Most Cyclists — Canadian soldiers overall — shared Captain George Scroggie's sentiment:

> I breathed a sigh of relief when the hour of the armistice arrived. We got back to Frameries that night and I had a hot bath and went to bed around 9 p.m. and slept soundly until 7 a.m., when I was awakened by the noise of a babble of voices outside the windows of my room. There was a big project under way as the housewives of Frameries were washing the cobblestones of the main street of the town for the Prince of Wales was due to come to town that morning and was going to make a speech at the Town Hall of Frameries.[21]

Even though the war was over, the Cyclists and the rest of the Canadian Corps were not going home just yet.

Canadian armoured cars passing Saluting Base, Mons, Belgium, November 1918.

9

Occupying Force

The terms of the armistice that ended hostilities on November 11, 1918, allowed Allied armies to occupy Germany until specific terms to end the Great War could be negotiated. Invited to be part of the British occupying force, Currie selected the 1st and 2nd Canadian Divisions to represent Canada. British troops were to advance to the left bank of the Rhine River and occupy a series of bridgeheads at key crossings on the right bank between Düsseldorf and Bonn. The Canadians would hold the line between Bonn and Cologne, midway to Düsseldorf.

The 1st and 2nd Divisions set out on the 250-mile march from Mons to the Rhine on November 18, one day after special church services were held to celebrate Thanksgiving . (The 3rd and 4th Divisions remained in Belgium before moving back to England for demobilization.) The two Canadian divisions marched under operational conditions in various column strengths (one, two, or three depending on the terrain) along separate routes: the 1st Division headed for Cologne, the 2nd Division for Bonn.

As they had since the Pursuit from the Sensée the previous month, cavalry troops and Cyclists performed advance and flank patrol duties while on the march (sometimes up to a day in advance of the main column), and guard duty while encamped. "A" Cyclist Company was assigned to the 2nd Division[1] and "B" Company to the 1st Division.[2] Working with the latter, Cyclist Captain Dick Ellis recalled the march to the Rhine like this:

> On November 17th and 18th the first and second Canadian Divisions started for the Rhine. Orders were to proceed under active service conditions, all wearing steel helmets and officers carrying their revolvers. The cavalry provided a screen and guards and piquets had to be posted at night. In addition to the main advance guards, each unit had to provide its own, and platoons of cyclists were attached to various battalions for this purpose. It was not a very comfortable trip. The weather was generally bad and most of the roads hilly and rough. Moreover, the ASC were having some difficulty in keeping us fed and it is an old truism that an army marches largely on its stomach.[3]

A number of things struck the Canadians as they marched. One was the relatively pristine nature of the countryside — the ravages of the war had not extended much beyond the Belgian border. Another was the general lack of animosity of the local population, particularly as the Divisions marched into Germany in early December. According to Ellis,

> We crossed into Germany on December 4th and most of us actually felt more at home then because Anglo-Saxons have so many traits in common with Nordics and not having been touched by war, everything was clean and neat. At times we found it difficult to understand why we had been fighting the Germans who were generally passive to co-operative in their reception of us. In one billet some of the boys even had their clothes, boots and cycles cleaned for them. This was the home of the Stollwerchs, the chocolate kings of Germany. Good treatment paid off, of course, because if any of the Germans went to the

opposite extreme and tried to hold out on us, we soon showed them who had won the war.[4]

Another thing the Canadians encountered as they marched were Allied prisoners of war recently released by German forces. According to Captain Dick Ellis, "No transportation had been arranged for them and hitch-hiking facilities were not very good going west. Many of them were in a pitiful condition. We could only hope that when they got behind our columns they would be well taken care of."[5] Two POWs who were fortunate to make their way back were Privates W. Oborne and A.B. Wardell of "B" Cyclist Company, No. 4 Platoon.

POWs

Back in October, Oborne and Wardell had been working as runners for the 44th CIBn. On October 31, the two were instructed to take a message from Maing to CIBn HQ, 500 yards outside Famars. About 300 yards from the village, Wardell (in the lead) and Oborne hit a stretch of wet pavés and fell off their bikes. Wardell described what happened next: "On looking round to see if Osbourne [sic] was coming, I saw eighteen or twenty Germans come out of a house behind him, with fixed bayonets. At the same time, six or more came at us from the opposite side of the road."[6]

As runners, the two were not carrying rifles, so surrendered, whereupon they were escorted to a small village two miles behind enemy lines. Here they were questioned "as to the guns, tanks etc. behind our lines and if an attack was pending." The two claimed to have answered "I do not know'" to all questions, telling their interrogators they were "new men" who "did not know anything at all." The Germans apparently also questioned the two "about Cyclists, not having heard of them previously."[7]

Oborne and Wardell were shuffled around to various other locations for interrogation, first to Mons for a couple days, then forced to walk "six kilometres to a big concentration camp on the eastern outskirts of Mons."[8] After three days of questioning there, the pair were marched to

Soignies, then taken by train to Brussels, and finally to Maransart, where they stayed until November 11. They were "not told the Armistice was signed and on the 11th were hitched twenty to a heavily loaded wagon and started eastwards toward Germany. We travelled about twenty kilometres a day, drawing the loaded wagons."[9]

As with many POWs, Oborne and Wardell were given little food and had to fend for themselves, sometimes at their peril. According to Wardell:

> I did not get enough food at any time and what I did get was of poor quality. On the 12th November while drawing the loaded wagons and passing through a small town, the townspeople were giving us food and apples. I left the ranks with some others to get these and just as I got away a few yards, I was struck twice with the butt of a rifle, in the back and leg.[10]

While pulling the wagons on the morning of November 14, Oborne and Wardell learned the war was over "when a German orderly rode up on his cycle and gave the officer commanding a note and we were at once released on the road. We were told in English via the interpreter to get back to England the best way we could, also saying he was through with us and we would get no more food. We were given no rations on release."[11]

Without money or food, Oborne and Wardell walked to Brussels, arriving on November 17. There, they stayed with private families who treated them "exceptionally well." On the 22nd, the pair walked to Ghent, where they hitched a ride with British lorries travelling to Ostend. From there, they boarded a destroyer bound for Dunkirk, took the train to Calais, and eventually travelled by ship back to Dover at the beginning of December.

PATROL DUTY

In typical fashion, there was some competition between the 1st and 2nd Canadian Divisions as to who would reach the Rhine first. As the most senior division, troops with the 1st Division expected to have bragging rights.[12] On December 6, however, 1st Division troops found out the 2nd Division was "out to beat them" when reports came in from advance patrols that the 2nd had crossed into Germany a full day ahead of when the 1st was planning to cross.[13] Working as advance guard for the 3rd CIBn, No. 4 Cyclist Platoon "put on steam"[14] and were successful in being the first platoon to reach the Rhine at 08:00 on December 9 at the Main Bridge in Cologne.[15]

As the two divisions arrived and settled in to their positions over the next few days, preparations began for the official crossing of the Rhine on the Kaiser Wilhelm Bridge on December 13. According to Cyclist Jack Farquhar, the crossing "was to have been a big show but pouring rain dampened it considerably. The Cyclists did not go over in a body, being still split up and attached to various battalions." Despite the rain, senior Allied dignitaries were on hand to take salute from troops as they marched by, General Herbert Plumer (commander of the British Second

Canadian Light Horse passing Saluting Base on Bonn Bridge, December 1918.

Army) in Cologne and General Currie in Bonn. Farquhar recalls his experience in Cologne:

> Part way across the bridge Gen. Plumer was sitting on a white horse taking the salute. I called the platoon to attention and saluted. Gen. Plumer then called me over and said to let the boys stand on one side of him and see a sight they would most likely never see again. We all moved over beside the General and the 16th Battalion marched on to the bridge; the sun came out for a few moments just then and it was a wonderful sight to see the rain drops glistening on the bayonets and the kilts swinging to the pipers playing "Cook of the North." I wouldn't have missed that sight for anything in this world.[16]

Once across the Rhine, the Cyclists performed a number of light duties, including manning "control posts on the road marking the boundary between the British and US troops who were stationed next to us up the river. The powers-that-be may have feared a repetition of the fights that had occurred at times when Canadians and Australians

Cyclists crossing Cologne.

started bragging about their respective capabilities after indulging in too much beer or wine. However, only the odd Yank came in sight and no trouble developed."[17] The Cyclists continued in these roles before being moved to Battalion HQ in Endenich, a suburb of Bonn, on December 21.

HOME

At the end of January 1919, the Canadian Cyclists began the long trek home. From Endenich, they travelled back to Belgium, where they "turned in [their] cycles, machine guns, transport and all ... heavier stores and equipment." Then it was a 48-hour train ride to Le Havre "in the famous 8 cheveaux — 40 hommes boxcars."

Officers, Canadian Corps Cyclist Battalion, January 1919. Reprinted in the *Toronto Star*, April 23, 1919, with this caption: "Top row, left to right: Lt. W.A. Kyle, Lt. GHS Bell, Lt. S. Thompson, Lt. L. Henderson, Lt. W. Game, Lt. W. Baines, Capt. Geo. E. Scroggie, MC. Bottom row, left to right: Capt. F. Power, Capt. R.B. Cameron, M.C. Major A.E. Humphrey, D.C.O. (O.C.) Capt. E.V. McKague, Major A.E. Humphrey, D.C.O. (O.C.) M.C. Lt. Geo. Wilson, Lt. G. Crofton. Not present: Capt. F.G.C. Chadwick, M.C., Lt. L.D. Wilson, Lt. W.L. Wilson, Lt. J. Brown, Capt. Geo. E. Scroggie, MC."

Dick Ellis recalls it being "bitterly cold but at each stop the boys piled out to scrounge as much relief as possible. After one particularly rewarding sortie one box car wound up with a brazier, a bag of coal and a forty gallon keg of beer. No more misery that night: just happy songs to the tune of Stan Hunt's violin."[18] On March 2, the Cyclists boarded the *Duchess of Devonshire* for passage to Camp Witley back in England, where they were "decked out with new clothing and sent off on two weeks' leave with orders to report back at Ripon in Yorkshire, which was the departure point for Canada."[19]

In mid-April, the Cyclists boarded the *Adriatic* for passage back to Halifax.[20] The Cyclists, along with the 3rd and 4th Battalion Tunneling Companies, boarded trains for Toronto on April 22, arriving just before midnight.[21] The *Toronto Star* described the "Adventurous Careers" of the Cyclists like this in an April 1919 article:

> During the last two years of the war, no battalion had a more adventurous life than the cyclists. In many ways, this was compensation for the indescribably monotonous two years at the first when stationary trench warfare was the order of the day. The cyclists then were put at every conceivable kind of job from peeling potatoes to traffic control. When the change came, however, it came with a vengeance; and the Cycle Battalion, with the machine gunners so often their companions, were in the very front of the allied advance. As scouts, they kept in close touch with the retreating Boche. They were in the thick of the fighting at the Somme, Vimy, Passchendaele, Amiens, Arras, and all the subsequent fighting till the armistice, during which they suffered very heavy losses in reconnaissance brushes with enemy troops.[22]

Epilogue

The legacy of Canadian Cyclists in the Great War is based on and bound up with the pioneering contributions made by the Canadian Independent Force/Brutinel's Brigade to the Hundred Days campaign, specifically as they relate to the development of the Canadian Corps's combined arms strategy, mobile warfare doctrine, and consummate professionalism.

Brutinel's team was a microcosm of the Canadian Corps's combined arms efforts that featured so prominently in the Hundred Days campaign with the Cyclists working hand-in-glove with armoured cars, machine guns, trench mortars, cavalry, motorcycles, and engineers throughout the period. Currie and his commanders began developing this strategy over the winter of 1917–18 in anticipation of the need for coordinated battle-field efficiency in the impending Allied offensive. The strategy became "part of the largely unwritten attack doctrine of the Canadian Corps" at Amiens and after, acting "not only as a harbinger of what was to come in the future, but even hinted at the problems and advantages of modern 'mechanized' warfare theory."[1] It was this strategy — in Brutinel's words, "the necessity of close cooperation with the other Batteries and all Arms of the Service"[2] — that Brutinel and his commanders fine-tuned in the weeks prior to the assault on the Canal du Nord as part of their efforts to build the "broad and comprehensive Esprit de Corps" Brutinel thought was lacking at Amiens and Arras. The training paid off, perhaps most handsomely during the Pursuit from the Sensée, where Major-General Sir David Watson gave credit for the operation's "splendid results" to the "gallantry and vigour" of the co-operation in Brutinel's "Squadrons of Cavalry, the Cyclists and the Armoured Cars and affiliated Guns in Lorries with Crews" and between the infantry of Watson's 4th Division.[3]

Working as part of Brutinel's team, Canadian Cyclists also contributed to the evolution of the Canadian Corps's doctrine of mobile warfare in the Hundred Days. As military historian Shane Schreiber put it:

> [At Amiens,] Currie and Brutinel envisioned the Independent Force as a highly mobile unit capable of seizing and holding key terrain features in advance of the infantry, or as a means of dominating terrain with firepower until some means could be worked out to actually take and hold it. Their experiments put the Canadian Corps on the leading edge of developing a doctrine of "mechanized" warfare, albeit a primitive one. Currie's use of such an eclectic, *ad hoc* organization showed not only a flair for the innovative, but also a faith in his subordinates (in this case Brutinel) that would be well rewarded at battle's end.[4]

One of the Corps's first experiments with mobile warfare occurred in the Spring Offensive of 1918 with the deployment of the 1st CMMGB to support the British 5th Army, where, as one Cyclist recalled, it "moved hither and thither, all up and down the 5th Army front, wherever there was a break-through to be contained, or a gap in the line to be filled."[5] The scope of the experiment was expanded at Amiens with the addition of the Cyclists and trench mortars to the Canadian Independent Force in its efforts to help the French 31st Corps "keep pace with the momentous advance of the two Dominion corps to the north, and thereby ensuring that the Canadian Corps' flank was protected."[6] During the open warfare of the Pursuit from the Sensée, the Cyclists, along with cavalry, armoured cars, trench mortars, and machine gunners from Brutinel's brigade were "embedded" within the advancing 1st and 4th Canadian Divisions to keep contact with the enemy rearguard, providing a "forward screen" for the infantry brigades leapfrogging immediately behind them[7] — yet another contribution to the "splendid results" lauded by Major-General Watson.

Canadian Cyclists also displayed a remarkable degree of professionalism, a hallmark of the Canadian Corps as a whole. By the summer of 1918, the Corps — "its commanders, staff officers, and soldiers alike" — had become a "highly competent, experienced team" capable of designing and executing offensives with efficiency and to great success.[8] Historian Jack Granatstein put it this way in discussing the Corps's plans for Amiens:

> The staff planners who had spent weeks preparing the 12-inch thick tactical and administrative orders for the attack on Vimy Ridge in April 1917 now were skilled enough to devise complicated plans in days, and to do so without the paper burden that had previously been necessary…. The planners interpreted intelligence reports, and they prepared their plans to fit what they knew and what the Allied high command wanted. General Currie's Corps headquarters drew up the overall attack plan, laying down the tasks for each of the Corps' four divisions. At the division, plans were adjusted to fit each of the brigades, and the brigade staff passed orders to battalions. At the Amiens battle, for example, the 1st Canadian Infantry Brigade's orders covered only two pages.[9]

Despite the complexity of the engagements, the Cyclists' orders got shorter and less prescriptive over the Hundred Days campaign. While most orders included some specific objective, Canadian Cyclists, along with the rest of Brutinel's team, were given wide latitude to determine what was needed for success in the field. At Cambrai, Brutinel's Brigade was placed on standby with instructions to be ready to secure the bridges along the Canal de l'Escaut northeast of Cambrai and "take advantage of any opening to exploit success."[10] At the Canal du Nord, the brigade was instructed to "thicken up" machine gun barrages, "seize tactical features in advance of our Line and [hold] them until the arrival of the Infantry," participate in the Corps's general advance, and serve as rearguard — whatever was "required by the situation."[11] At the Sensée, Brutinel's force was instructed to "keep in constant touch with the enemy as it retreated and communicate enemy positions and anything else of importance like road and bridge status to the infantry coming behind."[12] For many of the Cyclists, the lack of specific instructions meant, as Cyclist Macnab recalled, "being out in advance most of the time [and never knowing] when we were going to run into trouble…. Sometimes it would be snipers; sometimes machine guns; sometimes field artillery using 'open sights,' that is, firing directly at us from positions in the open."[13] The level of training, experience, and mettle required for such fighting was exceptional. As author Tim Cook put it, fighting during this period "called for an exceptional degree of daring and resource." He continues:

> Front line men had not only to close with the enemy in circumstances of comparative isolation — that is, without the moral support of the old close order formation — but they had to think and co-operate skillfully with the other troops engaged alongside of them; there could be no more blind charging. "Cannon fodder" had to give place to a high type of disciplined manhood, if attacks, under the new methods, were to carry the day in the face of a determined enemy.[14]

Professionalism, hard-earned experience, careful training, and excellent leadership are what allowed Canadian Cyclists — Brutinel's team as a whole — to function so effectively with such little direction.

The Hundred Days campaign of the Great War proved once and for all that Lieutenant General Arthur Currie's Canadian Corps had evolved into an innovative, efficient, and highly professional fighting force, and that Canadian Cyclists made small but important contributions to that evolution. The legacy of the Canadian Cyclists in the Great

War came at a deadly cost: Out of a total enlistment of 1,138 men, 261 were killed or wounded — a casualty rate of 23 percent.[15]

In 1934, Canadian Cyclists gathered in Toronto for the first time since the Great War to commemorate those who did not return. They began by reading this portion of Major-General Archie Macdonell's *Final Order of the Day* to the 1st Canadian Division:

> This is a solemn time for us all.
>
> No Canadian can view the demobilization of the Canadian Corps and all that it means and stands for without emotion.
>
> We have been through great things together, seen much, endured much, and accomplished much. Memories crowd fast upon us; our victories, our glorious dead — who fell battling for the Right, and therefore, fell in the Peace of God, and live today as never before — our maimed and mutilated comrades, Canada's care and ours, through life.
>
> The Canadian Corps has proved on many a bloody, triumphant field that it is the last word in military efficiency — front line assault troops and uniformly successful.
>
> One does not know which branch or arm to praise most; all are so splendidly gallant, loyal and efficient, of proved worth and valour.
>
> Canada is proud of you and Canada is grateful. God bless and protect every one of you in the years to come and give you each Happiness and Success.
>
> Remember that we of the Canadian Corps stand present for the King.[16]

At a 1937 Cyclist reunion,[17] Dick Ellis — the unofficial guardian of the Cyclists' legacy after the war — donated a bottle of Pol Roger champagne to the Canadian Corps Cyclist Battalion Association and charged that it be drunk by its last two surviving members. Incredibly, Ellis himself shared that bottle with fellow Cyclist Billy Richardson in 1992. Richardson died in 1995, leaving Ellis the sole surviving member of the Canadian Corps Cyclist Battalion. Ellis died on August 14, 1996, at the very good age of 100.[18]

Bottle of Pol Rogers champagne donated to the Canadian Corps Cyclist Battalion Association by Captain Dick Ellis in 1937. The bottle was opened June 6, 1992, by the last two Canadian Cyclists, Dick Ellis and Billy Richardson.

Acknowledgements

I owe many thanks to librarians, archivists, and staff across the country for their assistance: Susan Ross, Fiona Anthes, Christina Parsons, and Carol Reid at the Canadian War Museum; Liz McQuaig at the Mississauga Library System; Shari Strachan and Vino Vipulanantharajah at the Musée Héritage Museum; staff at Archives of Ontario, City of Toronto Archives, Library and Archives Canada, and the Toronto Reference Library. Thanks also to Richard Law for contributing the Mil Art Images from his father's collection and Kate Jory for the fact-checking.

At Dundurn Press, thanks to Kirk Howard for believing in this project; Scott Fraser for setting a land-speed record in responding to the initial submission (and with such enthusiasm!); Allison Hirst for exceptional editing (those place names!); the design team for bringing the Cyclists to life again; Michelle Melski and her team for ensuring people know about the book; and everyone else at the Press who has and will contribute to the book's success.

To my wife, Sara, thanks for some time and space to focus on this project. To Wyatt Edward and C.R. Glenn, I look forward to reading all the books that you will write.

While *Riding into Battle* is the product of much collective assistance, any errors, omissions, or misinterpretations are my responsibility alone.

Notes

INTRODUCTION

1. The movement of over one hundred thousand troops and a massive supply chain through uncharted territory on two narrow, heavily congested roads was, in Schreiber's words, a "logistical triumph," a "small miracle" of planning and co-ordination executed on one day's notice. Shane Schreiber, *Shock Army of the British Empire* (Westport, CT: Praeger, 1997), 37.
2. W.D. Ellis and J. Gordon Beatty, *Saga of the Cyclists in the Great War, 1914–1918* (Toronto: Canadian Corps Cyclist Battalion Association), 67. Hereinafter cited as *Saga*.
3. On July 31, the Cyclists travelled from Wagonlieu, two and a half miles west of Arras, to Gézaincourt, just south of Doullens. On August 1, the Cyclists pedalled down the Gézaincourt–Candas road to Thieulloy-l'Abbaye via Candas, Fienvillers, Domart-en-Ponthieu, Airaines, and Camps-en-Amiénois.
4. *War Diary, Canadian Corps Cyclist Battalion*, September 1918, entry for August 1.
5. *Saga*, 53.
6. Wilfred Dancy "Dick" Ellis died in 1996, the last surviving member

of the 1st Canadian Corps Cyclist Battalion. Allan Barnes, "Dick Ellis, 100, Last Survivor of World War I Cyclists' Corp." *Toronto Star*, August 17, 1996: A6.

7. *Saga*, 67.

8. By August, the French were critically short of tanks and sacrificed the element of surprise in the initial stages of the battle for an artillery bombardment. Nicholson, 395.

9. Logan, Major H.T., Captain M.R. Levey, with Brig.-Gen. R. Brutinel, Major W.B. Forster, Lieut. W.M. Baker, Lieut. P.M. Humme, *History of the Canadian Machine Gun Corps, C.E.F.* (Bonn, London, Ottawa: Canadian War Narrative Section, 1919), 2. Hereinafter cited as *CMGC History*.

10. *Original Order*, 34.

11. *Original Order*, 32.

12. In anticipation, all units were instructed to carry three days' rations and ensure all water bottles were full. *Original Order*, 32.

13. *CMGC History*, 19.

14. Ibid.

15. Ibid.

16. *Saga*, 69.

17. Official War Diary, Diary of Events and Report on Work Performed by Nos. 1 & 2 Sections No. 5 Platoon Canadian Corps Cyclist Battalion, Re. Sheet 1/20000, p.50 (signed) Sgt F.C. Wingfield.

18. *Saga*, 69.

19. Ken Pettis, "History of the So-Called Fifth Divisional Company," in *Canadian Corps Cyclist Battalion Association, 1914–1918*, edited by John Moran (Toronto: The Association, 1941), 17. Pettis would go on to become RAF Squadron Leader in the Second World War.

20. *Saga*, 46.

21. Ibid., 20.

22. Lieut. W.M. Everall, "Precis written by Lieut. W.M. Everall, 1st Divisional Cyclist Co., July 1915, and submitted to HQ 1st CDN Division." *Cyclone* 3, Issue 8 (October 1970).

23. *Saga*, 10.

24. Ibid., 56.

25. Ibid., 58.
26. Ibid., 68.
27. *CMGC History*, 109.
28. Nicholson, 440.
29. *CMGC History*, 18.
30. Ibid., 22.
31. Ibid., 27.
32. *Saga*, 79–80.
33. *CMGC History*, 126.
34. Ibid., 36.
35. Ibid.
36. Ibid.
37. *War Diary, Canadian Corps Cyclist Battalion, of "B" Company, Appendix 'B,"* 16-11-18 to 21-12-18.
38. *Saga*, 82.
39. Capt. George Scroggie, "History of 'C' Company Canadian Corps Cyclist Battalion," *Cyclone* 3, Issue 1 (December 1965).
40. Not surprisingly, like many other units in the Canadian Corps, Cyclists often called themselves the "Suicide Squad." Unknown, "The 'Suicide Corps' Help Chase the Hun." *Toronto Daily Star*, September 13, 1918, 1.

CHAPTER 1: BATTLE OF THE HUMBER

1. *Saga*, 3.
2. Standard British practice was 16 battalions of 1,000 men each; battalions, in turn, contained four 225-man infantry companies, with companies having four platoons of about 50 men each, with chains of command through the ranks and divisional units which reported directly to divisional command.
3. "Mounted Troop" status quickly earned Canadian Cyclists the nickname "gas pipe chargers," a sobriquet especially popular amongst infantrymen. cefresearch.ca/wiki/index.php/ORBAT_1914.
4. FPU Croker, "The Man-Powered Military Vehicle," *The Army Quarterly and Defence Journal* 101, No. 4 (July 1971).

5. Bruce Gudmundsson, *The British Army on the Western Front 1916* (New York: Osprey Publishing, 2007), 36.

6. Ibid.

7. According to Wesley Cheney: "The most infamous draft-dodging, conscientious-objecting bicycle messenger you never knew you knew: Gefreiter Adolf Hitler. By the end of the First Battle of Ypres, Hitler's regiment had been reduced to 600 men, from the original 3,600. Hitler was promoted from Schtze (Private) to Gefreiter (Corporal), and assigned to the post of Radfahrer bis Regiment (Regimental Bicyclist.) It was as a bike messenger that Hitler would earn two Iron Crosses, and one of his Iron Crosses was at the recommendation of a Jewish officer. Ironically, though, as another blog has pointed out, Hitler's experience on a bicycle did not stop the Nazis from passing legislation to ban bikes from roads in favor of cars." Wesley Cheney, "Bikes at War Part Two: The Great War," bikeshophub.com/blog/2016/09/16/bikes-at-war-part-two-the-great-war. Accessed 2017-10-13.

8. Everall, "Precis Written by Lieut. W.M. Everall."

9. According to Bush and Delavigne, "About two weeks before the Division was due to sail, another bright lad from H.Q. got an idea (It is, of course, too much to hope that the first one could have had two ideas — he would have been immediately promoted to Lance-Corporal). He found that the Divisional complement called for a Company of Cyclists — and they didn't have any!" (6). Major Clayton E. Bush and C.S.M. Fred V. Delavigne, "History of the First Divisional Cyclist Company," in *Canadian Corps Cyclist Battalion Association, 1914–1918*, edited by W.D. Ellis (Toronto: The Association, 1950), 6.

10. Tim Cook, *At the Sharp End* (Toronto: Penguin Group, 2007), 36.

11. *Saga*, 4.

12. Ibid.

13. Ibid.

14. Ibid., 6.

15. Ibid.

16. J.L. Granatstein, *The Greatest Victory: Canada's One Hundred Days, 1918* (Don Mills: Oxford University Press, 2014), 54.

17. "Recent research suggests that … most elements of the division engaged in productive training on Salisbury Plain. The infantry learned to manoeuvre in conjunction with artillery and machine guns. Other divisional elements, such as engineers, artillery and signals, as well as mounted and transport troops carried out their own specialized programs. The engineers, for example, learned how to construct field fortifications, while the artillery brigades rehearsed their gun drills. The divisional transport and ammunition columns, meanwhile, discovered the intricacies of moving supplies around the battle zone." Unknown, "Canadian Training School in Shorncliffe," www3.nfb.ca/ww1/building-a-force-film.php?id=531245. Accessed 2017-10-13.

18. Bush and Delavigne, 7.

19. Ibid.

20. Ian Skennerton, "Pedal Power: The British Military Bicycle," *Arms & Militia Collector* 5, No. 2 (1991).

21. The bicycles initially supplied to Canadian Cyclists were Planets made by Planet Cycle Works on Toronto's Queen Street East, "one of the more popular and successful Toronto-based brands to come out of the 1890s bicycle boom."

    "The individual responsible for supplying the Canadian military with bicycles was none other than Tommy Russell, general manager and soon to be president of CCM. Following a meeting on August 14, 1914, with the minister of militia and defence, Colonel Sam Hughes, Russell was made an honorary Major and named purchasing agent for the Canadian Expeditionary Forces. Unknown, "Remembrance Day 2012," vintageccm.com/content/remembrance-day-2012-0. Accessed 2017-10-13.

22. Skennerton, Ian, "Pedal Power: The British Military Bicycle," *Arms & Militia Collector* 5, No. 2, 33 (1991). bsamuseum.wordpress.com/the-military-roadster. Accessed 2017-10-13.

23. Quoted in Skennerton, 36.

24. *Saga*, 53.

25. Ibid., 7.

26. Bush and Delavigne, 7.

27. *Saga*, 8.

28. Ibid., 14.

29. Ibid.

30. Ibid., 15.

31. Ken Baillie and A.A. Swinnerton, "History of the Second Divisional Cyclist Association," in *Canadian Corps Cyclist Battalion Association, 1914–1918*, edited by John Moran (Toronto: The Association, 1941), 8.

32. Unknown, "Realistic Battle Along Humber River," *The Globe*, March 25, 1915: 6.

33. Ibid.

34. Jock Farquhar, "Continuation of 'B' Company Story," *Cyclone* 2, Issue 12 (May 1959), 24.

35. *Saga*, 15.

36. Unknown, "Queen's Own Parades To Be Held During War," *The Globe*, April 15, 1915: 6.

37. Ibid.

38. Tomken is actually a portmanteau from the words *Thomas* and *Kennedy*.

39. William Davis, "Profile of Thomas Laird Kennedy," Ontario Archives. F 13-1, Container B410934.

40. Dovercourt Road, Lippincott Street, Denison Street, and Denison Square all owe their naming to the Denison family.

41. *Saga*, 19.

42. Ibid., 20.

43. Ibid.

44. Ibid.

45. Unknown, "Formation Of The 2nd And 3rd Divisions," Canada. yodelout.com/formation-of-the-2nd-and-3rd-divisions. Accessed 2017-10-13.

46. *Saga*, 19.

47. Ibid., 20. "After returning to the Company, Kennedy spent the fall in the trenches, but returned to Canada for operative treatment. His medical leave was extended a number of times until it was clear that he would not be returning to active duty and he was struck off strength with the rank of major in September 1917. He later attained the rank of colonel in the militia." Unknown, "Colonel Thomas Laird Kennedy,"

mississaugaatwar.wordpress.com/a-ck0114. Accessed 2017-10-13. Private Pengelly of the 2nd Division Cyclists remembered "no finer gentleman ever breathed" as Major T.L. Kennedy. Pengelly, "Huit Chevaux," *Cyclone* 3, Issue 5 (1968), 10.

48. Unknown, "Cyclists in Demand to Chase the Huns," *The Globe*, December 1, 1916: 6.

49. E.T. Heathcote, "History of the 3rd Divisional Cyclist Co.," *Cyclone* 2, Issue 7 (October).

50. *Saga*, 33.

51. Ibid.

52. Ibid.

53. Kelly, Tobias, 1941. "History of the Third Divisional Cyclist Association." In John Moran (ed.) *Canadian Corps Cyclist Battalion Association, 1914–1918* (Toronto: The Association, 1941), 11.

54. Scroggie, "History of 'C' Company Canadian Corps Cyclist Battalion."

55. *Saga*, 33.

56. "On another occasion," recalled Kelly, "it was our assignment to get within the lines at night, of the 35th Battalion at Port Credit. This was accomplished by hiring a farmer to drive us along the side road concealed in a box wagon, which had previously been used for hauling pigs. This was not the beginning of 'Gas Warfare,' but it was nearly the end of us. However, we reached our objective and caused quite a stir within the lines through liberal use of comparatively harmless explosives" (12).

57. Unknown, "Friday Manoeuvres of a Unique Nature," *Toronto Daily Star*, December 9, 1915: 2.

58. Ibid.

59. Kelly, 12.

60. Ibid.

61. Unknown, "Extracts from a Cyclists' Diary," *Cyclone* 2, Issue 17 (1962), 14–15.

62. Ibid., 15.

63. Ibid., 14.

64. According to Kelly: "As an item of meteorological interest, the snow [that] fell in England during February 1916 was much in excess of

the normal fall, so the Canadians felt much at home" (12).

65. "Extracts from a Cyclists' Diary," 14.

66. Ibid., 16.

67. *Saga*, 35

68. Ibid., 37.

69. Ellis, W., "History of the Fourth Divisional Cyclist Company," 14.

70. *Saga*, 37.

71. Unknown, "Many Cyclists in Sunday Run," *The Globe*, April 30, 1917: 13.

72. Ken Pettis, "History of the So-Called Fifth Divisional Company," 16.

73. Ibid.

74. Ibid.

75. Ibid., 17.

76. *Saga*, 47.

77. Ibid.

78. Pettis, 16–17. Incredibly, the motion picture Pettis references is called *The Division Cyclists* and can be viewed at this Library and Archives Canada site: youtube.com/watch?v=_wD-4uMjAzg.

79. Ibid., 18.

80. Unknown, "Cyclists in Demand to Chase the Huns," *The Globe*, December 1, 1916: 6.

81. Cook, *At the Sharp End*, 48.

82. Pettis, 17.

CHAPTER 2: THE TRENCHES

1. By the end of 1914, the French had suffered 800,000 casualties, the Germans 750,000, and Britain — who had only a small, professional army in Belgium at the outset of the war — 95,000. Cook, *At the Sharp End*, 66.

2. Ibid., 67.

3. Nicholson, 49.

4. Bush and Delavigne, 7.

5. *Saga*, 8.

6. Ibid.
7. Ibid.
8. Ibid.
9. Nicholson, 55.
10. *Saga*, 9.
11. Cook, *At the Sharp End*, 118.
12. *Saga*, 9.
13. Quoted in *Saga*, 9.
14. *Saga*, 10.
15. Ibid.
16. Brigadier Richard Turner, as quoted in Cook, *At the Sharp End*, 214.
17. *Saga*, 10.
18. Ibid.
19. In the British system of military organization, a corps is a "formation consisting of a permanent Headquarters, and usually from two to four Divisions." David Love, *A Call to Arms: The Organization and Administration of Canada's Military in World War One* (Winnipeg: Bunker to Bunker Books, 1999) 11.
20. *Saga*, 36.
21. Ibid., 40.
22. Ibid.
23. Ibid., 33.
24. Ibid., 39.
25. Ibid., 40–41.
26. Ibid., 44.
27. Ibid., 51.
28. *Cyclone* 2, Issue 8 (1956).
29. Scroggie, "History of 'C' Company Canadian Corps Cyclist Battalion."
30. *Saga*, 56.
31. Ibid., 62.
32. Nicholson, 250.
33. Ibid.
34. *Saga*, 60.
35. Ibid., 58.
36. Ibid., 59.

37. Ibid., 62.
38. Nicholson, 266.
39. Scroggie, "History of 'C' Company Canadian Corps Cyclist Battalion."
40. Ibid.

CHAPTER 3: AMIENS AND THE FULL POWER OF MANOEUVRE

1. Quoted in Nicholson, 386.
2. Schreiber, 47.
3. Earlier in the war, troops from "B" Company Cyclists were some of the first Canadian soldiers to see tanks in action during the Great War: "Some 'B' Company men played a part in guiding [the tanks] into position the night before by running sturdy white duck guide tapes about four to five inches wide in fan shape from their cleverly camouflaged park up to just behind the frontline. The Germans tried to stop them with rifle and machine-gun fire, bombs, heavy timbers and even bayonets, but only direct hits by shells worked. The two steering wheels at the rear of these first tanks were particularly vulnerable to shell fire." *Saga*, 56.
4. Schreiber, 35.
5. Cameron Pulsifer, "Canada's First Armoured Unit: Raymond Brutinel and the Canadian Motor Machine Gun Brigades of the First World War," *Canadian Military History* 10, Issue 1 (2012).
6. "There were 20 in all: eight armoured machine gun cars, which were the fighting nucleus of the unit, five trucks for carrying ammunition and supplies, four for transporting the officers, one for carrying gasoline, one repair truck, plus one ambulance, donated by the Autocar Company."
7. Pulsifer, 7.
8. Tim Cook, *Shock Troops* (Toronto: Penguin, 2008), 392.
9. *CMGC History*, Vol. 2, 74.
10. Unknown, "Brig.-Gen. Brutinel Dies in France," *Cyclone* (1962), 18.

11. Cook, *Shock Troops*, 393.

12. Nicholson, 383.

13. According to Nicholson: "The new 1st C.M.M.G. Brigade was formed from 'A' and 'B' Batteries (of the original M.M.G. Brigade), the Borden M.M.G. Battery and the 18th C.M.G. Company (from the 5th Division); the 2nd C.M.M.G. Brigade comprised the Eaton and Yukon M.M.G. Batteries, and the 17th and 19th C.M.G. Companies (5th Division)." (383).

14. Ludendorff quoted in Nicholson, 407.

15. Quoted in Nicholson, 408.

16. Quoted in *CMGC History*, Vol. 2, 9.

17. "Diary of Events and Report on Work Performed by No. 9 Platoon Canadian Corps Cyclist Battalion." Ref. Sheet Demulin 1/20000. P.43. (Signed) Lieut. G.E. Scroggie.

18. Tanks and their crews were not the only casualties at Amiens. While cavalry had been used throughout the war, it had become clear by the open warfare phase that marked the Hundred Days that their usefulness on the modern battlefield had passed. On August 10, a squadron of the Fort Garry Horse captured the village of Andechy, and after turning it over to French forces, continued their charge toward heavily-entrenched German defences. The squadron was slaughtered: it lost 112 horses and 45 all ranks that afternoon. Canadian Cyclists described the carnage a few days later on their move from Amiens to the Arras front: "The fields were littered with the bodies of dead Fort Garry and Strathcona Cavalry men and their horses."

19. Quoted in *CMGC History*, 106.

20. Nicholson, 415.

21. Ibid., 420.

22. *Saga*, 68.

23. Quoted in *CMGC History*, 109.

24. Ibid.

CHAPTER 4: ARRAS — A VERY DIFFICULT AND TIRESOME TASK

1. *CMGC History*, 1.
2. Ibid., 12.
3. *Saga*, 70.
4. Ibid., 70.
5. *CMGC History*, 117.
6. Nicholson, 434.
7. Ibid.
8. *CMGC History*, 118.
9. Nicholson, 436.
10. Ibid., 13.
11. Ibid.
12. Ibid., 15.
13. *War Diary, Canadian Corps Cyclist Battalion, September 1918*, entry for September 2.
14. *CMGC History*, 122.
15. Ibid.
16. Nicholson, 440.
17. *CMGC History*, 126.

CHAPTER 5: CANAL DU NORD — STICKY FIGHTING

1. Nicholson, 442.
2. Ibid.
3. Ibid., 441.
4. David Borys, "Crossing the Canal Combined Arms Operations at the Canal du Nord, September–October 1918," *Canadian Military History* 20, No. 4 (Autumn 2011), 23–38.
5. Nicholson, 443.
6. Schreiber, 110.
7. *CMGC History*, 126.
8. Ibid.

9.   Ibid.

10.   Ibid.

11.   Ibid.

12.   Ibid.

13.   Ibid.

14.   Ibid.

15.   Ibid.

16.   Ibid.

17.   Ibid.

18.   Ibid.

19.   Schreiber, 126.

CHAPTER 6: CAMBRAI — TAKE ADVANTAGE OF ANY OPENING

1.   *CMGC History*, 107.

2.   Ibid.

3.   According to Nicholson, "Construction of this position behind the two northern Groups of Armies had been ordered on 6 September, after the first big Allied offensive, but the required labour was not available before the last days of September. The Hermann Line branched off from the Flanders II Line (which ran from the Belgian coast at Nieuport to east of Roulers). It passed immediately west of Tournai, Valenciennes and Le Cateau, following successively stretches of the Scheldt, its tributary the Selle, and the upper Oise, before joining the Hunding-Brunhild position, constructed in 1917" (457).

4.   Nicholson, 458.

5.   Ibid, 453.

6.   *CMGC History*, 133.

7.   Ibid.

8.   Ibid.

9.   Ibid.

10.   *Saga*, 72–73. Already treated for "slight gassing" earlier in the war,

Mennill was extracted from the battlefield and treated for gun-shot wounds to the left thigh and right forearm. bac-lac.gc.ca/eng/discover/military-heritage/first-world-war/personnel-records/Pages/item.aspx?IdNumber=190821. Accessed 2017-10-13.

11.   W.G Smith, "Daily Report," *War Diary*, 1.

12.   *CMGC History*, 136.

13.   *Saga*, 72–73.

14.   Ibid., 75.

15.   Ibid., 75–76.

16.   Ibid., 77.

17.   *CMGC History*, 137.

18.   *Saga*, 79.

19.   Granatstein, 137.

20.   Schreiber, 110.

21.   Cook, *Shock Troops*, 548.

22.   Nicholson, 459–60.

23.   Granatstein, 85.

24.   *CMGC History*, 138.

25.   *Saga*, 79–80.

CHAPTER 7: PURSUIT FROM THE SENSÉE — THEIR "MOST TELLING WORK"

1.   *CMGC History*, 139.

2.   Nicholson, 467.

3.   Ibid.

4.   German High Command, in fact, had ordered forces to pull back to defensive positions on the Hermann Line on October 15. Nicholson, 468.

5.   *CMGC History*, 150.

6.   Ibid.

7.   Ibid.

8.   Schreiber, 118.

9.   *CMGC History*, 125.

10. *CMGC History*, 78.
11. *Saga*, 79–80.
12. *CMGC History*, 140.
13. Ibid.
14. *War Diary Appendix*. "C" Company, Attached to 4th Cdn Division, report for 18-10-18 to 24-10-18.
15. *CMGC History*, 140.
16. *War Diary Appendix*. "C" Company, Attached to 4th Cdn Division, report for 18-10-18 to 24-10-18.
17. *Saga*, 79.
18. Nicholson, 469.
19. Ibid.
20. *War Diary Appendix*. "C" Company, Attached to 4th Cdn Division, report for 18-10-18 to 24-10-18.
21. Ibid.
22. Nicholson has the 1st Division retiring on the 22nd, but *CMGC History* has it the evening of the 21st.
23. Nicholson, 469.
24. *War Diary Appendix*. "A" Company, Attached to 4th Cdn. Division, report for 18-10-18 to 24-10-18.
25. *Saga*, 79; *CMGC History*, 139.
26. *CMGC History*, 143.
27. Ibid.
28. Ibid., 36.
29. Ibid.

CHAPTER 8: VALENCIENNES AND MONS

1. Nicholson, 473. Nicholson notes: "The G.O.C. Canadian Corps Heavy Artillery later contrasted the weight of 2,149 tons of shells expended from noon on 31 October to noon on 2 November with the 2,800 tons fired by both sides in the whole South African War" (473).
2. *CMGC History*, 152.
3. Ibid.

4. *Saga*, 80.
5. *War Diary*, Report of "B" Company, Canadian Corps Cyclist Battalion, Attached 4th Cdn. Division, 28-10-18 to 6-11-18.
6. Cook, *At the Sharp End*, 568.
7. *CMGC History*, 153.
8. Ibid.
9. Nicholson, 475.
10. *CMGC History*, 158.
11. *Saga*, 81.
12. *CMGC History*, 156.
13. Ibid.
14. *War Diary*, Report of "B" Company, Canadian Corps Cyclist Battalion, Attached 4th Cdn Division, 28-10-18 to 6-11-18.
15. *CMGC History*, 156.
16. Ibid.
17. Nicholson, 479.
18. With the Independent Force for the first time, the two subsections of engineers carried with them over seven tons of timber for road and bridge repair. See *CMGC History*, 159.
19. Nicholson, 480.
20. *Saga*, 81.
21. Scroggie, "History of 'C' Company, Canadian Corps Cyclist Battalion," 25.

CHAPTER 9: OCCUPYING FORCE

1. No. 1 platoon to the 5th CIBn, No. 2 to the 4th, and No. 3 to the 6th.
2. No. 4 platoon to the 1st CIBn, No. 5 to the 2nd CIBn, and No. 6 to the 3rd CIBn.
3. *Saga*, 81.
4. Ibid., 82.
5. Ibid., 82.
6. No. 3130584 Statement by Pte Wardell, A.B., upon being repatriated from Enemy's lines.

7. No. 3130537 Statement by Pte Oborne, W., upon being repatriated from Enemy's lines.

8. Ibid.

9. Ibid.

10. No. 3130584 Statement by Pte Wardell, A.B., upon being repatriated from Enemy's lines.

11. No. 3130537 Statement by Pte Oborne, W., upon being repatriated from Enemy's lines.

12. *Saga*, 83.

13. Ibid.

14. Ibid.

15. *War Diary*, Canadian Corps Cyclist Battalion, of "B" Company, Appendix 'B," 16-11-18 to 21-12-18.

16. *Saga*, 83.

17. Ibid., 84.

18. Ibid.

19. Ibid.

20. Ibid.

21. Unknown, "Cyclists Are 1st Unit Home from Front," *Toronto Daily Star*, April 23, 1919: 4.

22. *Saga*, 84.

EPILOGUE

1. Schreiber, 62.

2. Ibid.

3. Ibid., 36.

4. Ibid.

5. Unknown, "Brig.-Gen. Brutinel Dies in France," *Cyclone* (1962), 18.

6. Schreiber, 50.

7. Ibid., 118.

8. Granatstein, 9.

9. Ibid.

10. *CMGC History*, 107.

11. Ibid.
12. *CMGC History*, 125.
13. *Saga*, 79–80.
14. Cook, *Shock Troops*, 404.
15. Scroggie, "History of 'C' Company Canadian Corps Cyclist Battalion."
16. Quoted in *Saga*, 85–86.
17. The Cyclists would continue to meet until 1983.
18. Barnes, A6.

A Note on Sources

The sources used in this book are like the layers of a painting. The first layer — the foundation — is based on G.W.L. Nicholson's *Official History of the Canadian Army in the First World War: Canadian Expeditionary Force 1914–1919*. His work provided the background on Canada's roles in the Great War and specific insight into the battles of the Hundred Days campaign.

The second layer of the painting is composed of the detailed roles performed by Canadian Cyclists in the Great War. This layer is derived from two main sources: the official war diaries of the various Cyclist units, especially those of the Canadian Corps Cyclist Battalion in the Hundred Days campaign, and the *History of the Canadian Machine Gun Corps, C.E.F.*, particularly Volume 3 for its rich and detailed history of the Canadian Independent Force/Brutinel's Brigade.

The insights and recollections of Cyclists themselves form the third layer of the book. These are based on publications by the Canadian Corps Cyclist Battalion Association, the most important of which are the battalion history published in 1941, the divisional Cyclist company histories published in 1950, various articles published in the *Cyclone*, the association's irregular bulletin published from 1934 to 1984, and

Dick Ellis and Gordon Beatty's 1963 *Saga of the Cyclists in the Great War, 1914–1918*, (primarily) Ellis's effort to collate and edit all previously published association sources into one single, coherent volume.

A fourth layer — much of the "colour" of the book — was derived from a variety of sources: newspaper accounts, especially the *Globe* and the *Toronto Star*; Archives Canada for the detailed war records referenced herein and the fantastic photographs included; Ontario Archives for Thomas Laird Kennedy's personal war diaries and photographs; and City of Toronto Archives for additional photographs, especially of Canadian Cyclists at Camp Exhibition and Paradise Grove, and for the 1916 film *The Divisional Cyclists: A Glimpse of a Day's Training* (see youtube.com/watch?v=_wD-4uMjAzg).

The fifth and final layer of the book, the analysis and insight that provides "finish" in key spots, comes from the following sources: Tim Cook's most excellent two-volume history of the Canadian Corps, *At the Sharp End: Canadians Fighting the Great War, 1914–1916* and *Shock Troops: Canadians Fighting the Great War, 1917–1918*; Shane Schreiber's poetic and insightful *Shock Army of the British Empire: The Canadian Corps in the Last 100 Days of the Great War*; and Jack Granatstein's *The Greatest Victory: Canada's One Hundred Days, 1918*.

One final note: except for metric used in direct quotes, all measurements are in imperial. As Granatstein put it, "Canadians during the Great War spoke and thought in yards and feet and measured speed in miles per hour. To translate these measurements into the metric system we used today, to my mind, would distort history."

Bibliography

Baillie, Ken, and A.A. Swinnerton. "History of the Second Divisional Cyclist Association." In *Canadian Corps Cyclist Battalion Association, 1914–1918*, edited by John Moran, Toronto: The Association, 1941.

Barnes, Allan. "Dick Ellis, 100, Last Survivor of World War I Cyclists' Corp." *Toronto Star*, August 17, 1996.

Borys, David. "Crossing the Canal Combined Arms Operations at the Canal du Nord, September–October 1918." *Canadian Military History* 20, No. 4 (Autumn 2011).

Bush, Major Clayton E., and C.S.M. Fred V. Delavigne. "History of the First Divisional Cyclist Company." In *Canadian Corps Cyclist Battalion Association, 1914–1918*, edited by W.D. Ellis, Toronto: The Association, 1950.

Cook, Tim. *At the Sharp End: Canadians Fighting the Great War, 1914–1916*. Toronto: Penguin Canada, 2007.

————.*Shock Troops: Canadians Fighting the Great War, 1917–1918*. Toronto: Penguin Canada, 2008.

Croker, F.P.U. "The Man-Powered Military Vehicle." *The Army Quarterly and Defence Journal* 101, No. 4 (July 1971).

Davis, William. "Profile of Thomas Laird Kennedy." Ontario Archives. F 13-1, Container B410934.

Ellis, W.D. "History of the Fourth Divisional Cyclist Company." In *Canadian Corps Cyclist Battalion Association, 1914–1918*, edited by John Moran. Toronto: The Association, 1941.

————, and J. Gordon Beatty. *Saga of the Cyclists in the Great War, 1914–1918*. Toronto: Canadian Corps Cyclist Battalion Association, 1965.

Everall, Lieutenant. "Precis written by W.M. Everall, 1st Divisional Cyclist Co. July 1915, and submitted to HQ 1st CDN Division." *Cyclone* 3, Issue 8 (October 1970).

Farquhar, Jock. "Continuation of 'B' Company Story." *Cyclone* 2, Issue 12 (May 1959).

Granatstein, J.L. *The Greatest Victory: Canada's One Hundred Days, 1918*. Don Mills: Oxford University Press, 2014.

Gudmundsson, Bruce. *The British Army on the Western Front 1916*. New York: Osprey Publishing, 2007.

Heathcote, E.T. "History of the 3rd Divisional Cyclist Co." *Cyclone* 2, Issue 7 (October 1955).

Kelly, Tobias. "History of the Third Divisional Cyclist Association." In *Canadian Corps Cyclist Battalion Association, 1914–1918*, edited by John Moran. Toronto: The Association, 1941.

Logan, Major H.T., Captain M.R. Levey, with Brig.-Gen. R. Brutinel, Major W.B. Forster, Lieut. W.M. Baker, Lieut. P.M. Humme. *History of the Canadian Machine Gun Corps, C.E.F.* Bonn, London, Ottawa: Canadian War Narrative Section, 1919.

Love, David. *"A Call to Arms": The Organization and Administration of Canada's Military in World War One*. Winnipeg: Bunker to Bunker Books, 1999.

Nicholson, G.H.L. *Official History of the Canadian Army in the First World War: Canadian Expeditionary Force 1914–1919*. Ottawa: Queen's Printer and Controller of Stationery, 1962.

Pengelly. "Huit Chevaux." *Cyclone* 3, Issue 5 (1968).

Pettis, Ken. "History of the So-Called Fifth Divisional Company." In *Canadian Corps Cyclist Battalion Association, 1914–1918*, edited by John Moran. Toronto: The Association, 1941.

Pulsifer, Cameron. "Canada's First Armoured Unit: Raymond Brutinel and the Canadian Motor Machine Gun Brigades of the First World War." *Canadian Military History* 10, Issue 1 (2012).

Schreiber, Shane. *Shock Army of the British Empire: The Canadian Corps in the Last 100 Days of the Great War.* Westport, CT: Praeger, 1997.

Scroggie, Capt. George. "History of 'C' Company Canadian Corps Cyclist Battalion." *Cyclone* 3, Issue 1 (December 1965).

Skennerton, Ian. "Pedal Power: The British Military Bicycle." *Arms & Militia Collector* 5, No. 2 (1991).

Unknown. "Brig.-Gen. Brutinel Dies in France." *Cyclone* 2, Issue 17 (1962), 18.

———. "Condensed History of the Canadian Corps Cyclist Battalion." In *Canadian Corps Cyclist Battalion Association, 1914–1918*, edited by John Moran. Toronto: The Association, 1941.

———. "Cyclists Are 1st Unit Home from Front," *Toronto Daily Star,* April 23, 1919.

———. "Cyclists in Demand to Chase the Huns." *The Globe,* December 1, 1916.

———. "Extracts from a Cyclists' Diary." *Cyclone* 2, Issue 17 (1962).

———. "Friday Manoeuvres of a Unique Nature." *Toronto Daily Star,* December 9, 1915.

———. "Many Cyclists in Sunday Run." *The Globe,* April 30, 1917.

———. "Queen's Own Parades to Be Held During War." *The Globe,* April 15, 1915.

———. "Realistic Battle along Humber River." *The Globe,* March 25, 1915.

———. "The 'Suicide Corps' Help Chase the Hun." *Toronto Daily Star,* September 13, 1918.

War Diaries. 1st Canadian Divisional Cyclist Company = 1914/10/12–1916/05/14. File. RG9-III-D-3.

———. 2nd Canadian Divisional Cyclist Company = 1914/10/15–1916/05/12. File. RG9-III-D-3.

———. 3rd Canadian Divisional Cyclist Company = 1916/03/24–1916/05/11. File. RG9-III-D-3.

———. Canadian Corps Cyclist Battalion = 1916/05/12–1919/03/31. File. RG9-III-D-3.

———. Canadian Reserve Cyclist Company = 1915/05/01–1919/02/28. File. RG9-III-D-3.

Image Credits

Bicycling World and Motorcycle Review: 28.

Canadian War Museum: 52, 53, 144.

City of Toronto Archives fonds 1244: 32 (bottom), 33 (bottom), 35 (bottom), 38.

Crowle Art Group: 14, 75, 87, 96.

© Government of Canada. Reproduced with the permission of Library and Archives Canada (2017): 18.

© Government of Canada. Reproduced with the permission of Library and Archives Canada (2017). LAC/Ministry of the Overseas Military Forces of Canada fonds/e001131472: 26, 32–33 (top), 40–41 (top and bottom), 42.

History of the Canadian Machine Gun Corps, C.E.F.: 119.

Library and Archives Canada/Ministry of the Overseas Military Forces of Canada fonds/e001131472: 35 (top), 43, 44, 46–47 (top and bottom), 48, 49, 50, 55, 61, 71, 72, 76, 78 (top and bottom), 79, 83, 84 (top and bottom), 88, 89, 97, 98 (top and bottom), 111, 115, 122, 127, 129, 134, 136.

McLellan, David, Imperial War Museums: 92 (top and bottom).

MilArt Photo Archives: 15, 29.

Mississauga Library System: 36, 37.

Musée Héritage Museum: 20.

National Library of Scotland, acc.3155: 135.

Nicholson: 13, 109.

Index

BOOK CREDITS

Acquiring Editor: Scott Fraser
Editor: Allison Hirst
Project Editor: Elena Radic
Proofreader: Tara Tovell

Cover Designer: Laura Boyle
Interior Designer: Jennifer Gallinger
E-Book Designer: Carmen Giraudy

Publicist: Michelle Melski

DUNDURN

Publisher: J. Kirk Howard
Vice-President: Carl A. Brand
Editorial Director: Kathryn Lane
Sales Manager: Synora Van Drine
Publicity Manager: Michelle Melski

Editorial: Allison Hirst, Dominic Farrell, Jenny McWha, Rachel Spence, Elena Radic
Design and Production: Laura Boyle, Carmen Giraudy
Marketing and Publicity: Kendra Martin, Kathryn Bassett

dundurn.com   dundurnpress
@dundurnpress   dundurnpress
dundurnpress   info@dundurn.com

FIND US ON NETGALLEY & GOODREADS TOO!

DUNDURN